Sacred SEDITION

Sacred SEDITION

Sinful
  Pursuit
of God

DWIGHT J. OLNEY

SACRED SEDITION
Copyright © 2014 by Dwight J. Olney

Unless otherwise indicated, all Scripture quotations are taken from the Holy Bible, New Living Translation, copyright ©1996, 2004, 2007 by Tyndale House Foundation. Used by permission of Tyndale House Publishers, Inc., Carol Stream, Illinois 60188. All rights reserved.

Scripture quotations marked (NASB) are taken from the NEW AMERICAN STANDARD BIBLE®, Copyright © 1960, 1962, 1963, 1968, 1971, 1972, 1973, 1975, 1977, 1995 by The Lockman Foundation. Used by permission.

Scripture quotations marked (KJV) are taken from the Holy Bible, King James Version, which is in the public domain.

ISBN: 978-1-4866-0218-6

Word Alive Press
131 Cordite Road, Winnipeg, MB R3W 1S1
www.wordalivepress.ca

WORD ALIVE PRESS
Just Write!

Cataloguing in Publication may be obtained through Library and Archives Canada

This work is humbly dedicated to Kristen, Jared and Heather, my three dear children who are the spice of my life, a fun reflection of their parents and a testament to the goodness of God.

CONTENTS

ACKNOWLEDGMENTS

It takes a village to raise a child and a community of helpful souls to write a book. I am deeply grateful for the kindness of the following people who came alongside me and contributed so generously to this project: Terry Wolverton for asking the question that started the ball rolling; the many friends who encouraged me to push on with the idea; Dr. Carl Hinderager, for scrutinizing the first draft; Dr. Joel From, for cleaning up my *Wrong* chapter; my daughters Kristen Schranz and Heather Olney, for proofreading the second draft; my wife Jeanette, for proofreading and editing the final draft; Lori Mackay, for putting the final polishing touches on the manuscript; and all the understanding folk at Word Alive Press, who graciously put up with the whining and quirkiness of authors in labor birthing their literary babies.

Question

SEDITION.

It's a nasty word.

Dictionaries define it as the act of stirring up resistance or rebellion against an authority. When I hear the word, I think of defiant and disloyal people who participate in mutinous, riotous or subversive activities—people like Lenin overthrowing Tsarist Russia in 1917 or fundamentalist Islamic terrorists bringing down the World Trade Center.

I've been called a lot of things in my life, but never seditious. It's no surprise. On the surface, I don't appear very rebellious. In fact, I'm fairly mild-mannered and playful by nature. I like to get along with people and to make rough waters smooth.

As I said, on the surface I don't look like a rebel. But there's a lot more to a person than just the surface.

I was raised in a Christian home. As a young lad, life was black and white. There were two kinds of people in the world—Christians and non-Christians.

As a Christian, I never thought of myself as superior to non-Christians, just more fortunate. I was glad that I had a desire to pursue God. I felt sad that many of my friends didn't. Being spared the horrors of alcoholism, marital breakup and the like, I could see the practical benefits of living a life of Christian morality. But for years I never really understood what it meant to know God intimately.

I prayed. I read my Bible from cover to cover, several times. I even went to Bible college for four years. But like many Christians, my spiritual life consisted of *me living my life for God.* Although that credo may sound right, there are two problems with it—and they both start with the letter *m.* When I base my search for a meaningful relationship with God on *me, my* thoughts and *my* efforts, there will always be deficiencies.

You see, I am a part of creation, not the Creator. And because creation is fallen, anything that is directed by me will have flaws. Consequently, the notion of *me living my life for God* will be stained with hypocrisy. To be honest, what that phrase really meant for me was a pursuit of God limited to my own desires. I was willing to offer God portions of my life but maintained control of the parts that were dominated by sin.

Basically I believed I could pursue God in my own fashion. Oh, I would have never expressed it that way out loud, but that is how I lived. And I fear that is how many other sincere God-seekers live as well. They have a desire to follow after God, but not necessarily in the manner that he prescribes. They are quite convinced they can find their own path to the Almighty.

The default setting of the natural mind is independence from God. So, even those with a desire to know God must be mindful of the temptation to pursue him according to their own plans. This all started to come together in my mind one night about two years ago when a friend of mine asked me the question—*Is it ever right to disobey God in order to be closer to God?*

At first I thought it was a silly question. Who would ever do that?

But as we talked, I came to realize that this was actually one of the most important questions I'd ever been asked in my life. It opened my mind to a whole new way of examining spiritual behavior, thereby creating a new paradigm for understanding the proper pursuit of God. This book is the culmination of what started that night.

I am fully convinced. Many people actually disobey God in their attempts to be closer to him. For the sake of our discussion, I have named this practice *sacred sedition.* It's sacred because it involves the pursuit of God. It's seditious because that pursuit is executed contrary to God's instructions.

Garden

IT ALL STARTED IN THE GARDEN.

The Creator had completed his work. Creation rested peacefully in communion with its maker. All the pieces were in place, all the parameters set and all the players were acting out their appropriate roles. The woman loved God and enjoyed her relationship with him. Every day, in the cool of the evening, she and her husband would commune with the Lord in harmonious bliss. There were no regrets. There was no shame.

Then the question came. *"Did God really say you must not eat the fruit from any of the trees in the garden?"* (Genesis 3:1). By misquoting God, a seed of doubt was planted. Maybe God was not as good as she thought.

As the woman dialogued with her tempter, she clarified the true nature of the arrangement—only the tree of the knowledge of good and evil was forbidden. But in the discussion that ensued, her trust in God began to erode. Perhaps he was holding out on her. What if there was something better for her beyond what God had commanded?

If the question had come with an air of anger or rebellion, it may have been less alluring. But it had all the flavor of a sound and benevolent theological statement—*in addition to what God has revealed, there is another way for hungry seekers to get closer to him.*

And the question came from such a shrewd creature. The line of reasoning sounded intelligent, not at all evil. Actually, it made good sense. The more the woman exercised her human reasoning, the more unreasonable the restriction seemed. This divine deprivation was perhaps an oversight on God's part.

And besides misquoting God, the tempter offered an express lane to an impeccable connection with the Creator. Being close to God felt so good. How could moving even closer be bad?

The lie was powerful because it fed the woman's deepest desire—to know God even more intimately. She was living according to his instructions, and life was great. But what if there was more to be experienced? What would that be like—to be just like God, to know everything as he knows it, both good and evil? Surely that would mean a deeper relationship with the Creator. That would be a good thing, right?

And so she ate.

Thus began the pattern of sacred sedition—disobeying God in an attempt to be closer to God.

Legacy

NOT ONLY DID EVE'S LEGACY SHOW UP IMMEDIATELY in the story, but it played a prominent role in the lives of many characters in the biblical narrative.

The woman's firstborn took after his mom. It was time to offer worship to the Lord. Baby brother obediently brought lambs, but Cain brought something from his own repertoire, apparently something outside of what God had prescribed. God rejected the attractive yet improper sacrifice but gave the older boy a chance to repent and do the proper thing. There was no mystery. He knew how to make things right.

But instead of humbly submitting to God's way, Cain flew into a rage over the fact that he was not allowed to pursue God in his own fashion. The humiliation angered him fiercely. How was this little brother of his a better man than he? He was the older and wiser of the two. He had always been the responsible one. Farming was hard work, a lot harder than watching a few sheep. Certainly he had the brains and the ability to come to God in a way that made sense to him. So passionate was Cain about his own religion that he even murdered for his cause.

Some crazy things have been done in the name of pursuing God outside the realm of his directives. At one point in the story, all of mankind disregarded God's command to fill the earth and congregated on the plains of Babylon to build a massive city with a tower that soared high into the sky. The structure, built with their own hands out of their own imaginations, was intended to be a huge monument to their own greatness. Their desire for intimate fellowship with God coupled with their passion for human significance created a twisted inner spiritual need. The Tower of Babel was created as a solution to meet that need. The sin in this story is not so much in the structure itself but in the characters' desire to live in a way that was different from what God had intended for them at that time.

In the story of Job, the friends who came to encourage the suffering saint arrived with a faulty philosophy of pursuing God, one limited to their own personal understanding of how God works. They were quite convinced that one could not suffer hardship and enjoy a pure relationship with God at the same time. According to their theology, suffering automatically meant sin in your life. But their theology was wrong.

In the end, God informed the friends that they had spoken wrongly about him. *They* were the ones who needed to repent, not Job. In fact, it was only Job's intercessory prayers that allowed them to escape the judgment of God. These friends had made a big mistake regarding the matter of getting to know God more intimately, and they had done so essentially by adding their own ideas to the truths of God.

Even Abraham, before he came through as the champion of Old Testament faith, fell to the temptation of pursuing God via human scheming. By all appearances, Abraham wanted to be a genuine follower of God. His first priority was to know God and be close to him. He even left the comfort of his homeland, the center of human civilization, to go to the outback land of Canaan because he believed God's promises for a son and a spectacular national future.

But as the years passed and the angst grew surrounding the absent promised heir, Abraham executed a definitive human move, totally outside of God's plan. He impregnated his wife's maid. But notice—this was not a man acting in rebellion or anger. This was a human being who wanted everything that God had for him. This was a guy who desired to hold tightly to his Lord.

With utmost sincerity, Abraham disobeyed God in order to be closer to him—classic sacred sedition. He was not intentionally rebelling against

God or running away from him. Truth be told, he probably considered his actions to be a way to help God out of a jam by providing a human solution to Sarah's passed expiration date. The result? Ishmael and millennia of conflict between Arabs and Jews.

When Abraham chose to sleep with Hagar rather than remain faithful to his wife and patient with God, he chose to sin in hope of improving his relationship with God. He pursued God apart from God's instructions. Such actions, no matter how sincere or genuinely heartfelt, take us not closer to God but to places where God ends up more distant.

Two generations later, the same pattern continued. Jacob had the call of God on his life to be the righteous influence in the lineage of the chosen people. But he chose to lead through human conniving and trickery. First he took advantage of Esau's great hunger to snatch the birthright away from his older brother. Then, with the help of his dysfunctional mother, Jacob tricked his blind and dying father into giving him the blessing that rightfully belonged to Esau.

When you read the text, you get the feeling that Jacob wanted to be a man of God, desiring to know him intimately and to be obedient to him. And yet for years, his modus operandi was one of deceit, clearly outside the realm of God's ideal plan.

Even the heroic figures in Israel's history needed time to figure out how to pursue God properly. Taught to fear Yahweh in his mother's arms, Moses was an Israelite through and through. Though raised and educated as an Egyptian, he sensed God's call to deliver the Israelites from slavery, out of the hands of their Egyptian oppressors. But instead of waiting for God's instructions on the liberation logistics, Moses ran ahead of the divine plan with a human strategy of his own—murder. Here is a man who loved God but justified killing another human being as a way to fulfill God's will and purposes. The next forty years of his life were spent tending sheep and figuring out what the true voice of God sounded like.

Later on in the story of the Exodus, Moses' brother pulled a legendary stunt that has stood for twenty-four centuries as a prime illustration of this ridiculous human propensity to pursue God in ways he never intended. While Moses was receiving the Ten Commandments on Mount Sinai, Aaron led the children of Israel into a blatant act of idolatry, outright rebellion that he claimed was actually honoring to God.

Remember the story? Moses was taking too long. The Israelites got impatient and begged Aaron for some spiritual leadership. His solution was the golden calf. Now if that wasn't bad enough, Aaron declared that this human idea was holy. Notice what he said in Exodus 32:5–6.

Aaron saw how excited the people were, so he built an altar in front of the calf. Then he announced, "Tomorrow will be a festival to the Lord!" The people got up early the next morning to sacrifice burnt offerings and peace offerings. After this, they celebrated with feasting and drinking, and they indulged in pagan revelry.

So they indulged in pagan revelry and called it a festival to the Lord.

I wonder if Samson used the same logic in his spiritual life, freely mixing God's purposes with his human passions. He was a political judge appointed by God to deliver the chosen people from the oppression of the Philistines. Samson was commissioned to do divine work, but he tried to be a man of God while maintaining personal sexual dalliances on the side. Such duplicity eventually led to his demise.

During the time of the judges, it was not uncommon for the people of God to invent their own strategies for pursuing God. After the Lord's miraculous delivery of Israel from the Midianites, Gideon properly resisted the people's request to make him their king. Gideon knew this was not part of God's plan, so he said, *"I will not rule over you, nor will my son. The Lord will rule over you!"* (Judges 8:23). But then he immediately proceeded to collect gold earrings from everyone in order to fashion a huge idol that he erected in his hometown for public worship. And as Judges 8:27 says, *"soon all the Israelites prostituted themselves by worshiping it, and it became a trap for Gideon and his family."* What happened here? Did this sudden surge of success in Gideon's spiritual life cause him to go soft in the head?

It appears King Saul had the same problem. He started off very well but then quickly veered off course. In his mind, he was convinced he could come to God and deal with spiritual matters on his own terms. Showing gestures of wanting to follow God, Saul ended up favoring ritualistic religiosity above simple obedience to the divinely revealed Word of God. *"Obedience is better than sacrifice"* (1 Samuel 15:22) came the message. Under the guise of relationship with God, Saul really just wanted to do his own thing.

Such was the case with the religious leaders of the day in the New Testament era. The Pharisees' all-time favorite topic was God. And yet for all their stringent codes and moral legalism, they were not even close to him. It was the same for the Sadducees. According to their benevolent human logic, all God really wanted was some good moral living in the here and now—no Kingdom of God, no resurrection. These so-called spiritual leaders thought they were tracking God, but they didn't even have him on the radar because their spiritual lives were humanly fabricated.

That's probably how the apostle Paul felt about his life before he was confronted by Christ on the road to Damascus—a lot of religion and very little real truth, a lot of pursuing God wholeheartedly according to human ideas. On paper, his list of religious credentials was impressive. But compared to the value of truly knowing Christ, Paul equated his resumé to a piece of garbage (Philippians 3:8). That is the true worth of human pursuits of God contrary to God's instructions.

The apostle Peter learned that lesson when he reprimanded Christ for talking about his upcoming death and resurrection (Matthew 16:21–23). Peter was feeling very religious at that moment—he had just made his bold proclamation that Jesus was *"the Messiah, the Son of the living God"* (Matthew 16:16). But when he ventured off on his own thoughts, as opposed to staying in tune with God, he was scolded for being an instrument of Satan. An eager believer can one moment proclaim truth and then the next proclaim a lie. Peter's problem at that second moment was that he was *"seeing things merely from a human point of view, not from God's"* (16:23).

Even when miraculous displays are abundant, the true work of God may not be present if such miracles are not part of a specific and deliberate divine plan. Such was the case with Simon the Sorcerer as recorded in Acts 8. Simon was a false teacher, but he was also a miracle worker with a reputation for being a great and powerful man of God. Under the sovereign conviction of God and through his connection with the evangelist Philip, Simon eventually became a believer. But when he saw the power of the Holy Spirit being manifested in the lives of the apostles, he asked if he could purchase some of this attractive divine magic. In his perverted mind, he was more in love with power than with Jesus. He was more interested in mesmerizing people than in walking obediently with the Savior. In all fairness to the man, once rebuked for his wickedness, Simon repented. He cried out for the apostles to pray for him so that he wouldn't be punished for his sin.

From this story, we learn that it's possible for one's heart to be *"not right with God"* in the midst of hungering for God. It's possible to have *"evil thoughts"*, be *"full of bitter jealousy"* and be *"held captive by sin"*, all in the mix of pursuing God (see Acts 8:20–23).

Mistaken

SO WHAT IS THE COMMON THREAD IN THESE STORIES we have just examined?

All these people thought they were genuinely pursuing God—and they were all wrong. But notice, these were not pagans who were rejecting relationship with God. These were people making gestures to move closer to him. They wanted to be the good guys. They were honest, sincere, God-seeking people, hunting for a deeper connection with the Almighty. But they were trying to do so not according to God's design but according to their own methods that they considered to be right in their own eyes. They were each practicing a form of sacred sedition.

Certainly, our Creator wants us to pursue him. *"Search for the Lord and for his strength; continually seek him"* (Psalm 105:4). *"Seek the Lord while you can find him"* (Isaiah 55:6). *"I would not have told the people of Israel to seek me if I could not be found"* (Isaiah 45:19).

Seeking God passionately is the right desire, but there are divine guidelines to keep us from going off track in this pursuit. Each drama cited in the past chapter showcased characters who were passionate for God but believed they could achieve greater intimacy with him through humanly devised methods. At the risk of sounding cliché, it's one of those *sincere, but sincerely wrong* situations.

I suppose that is the simplest explanation for the origin of every false religion in the world. Humans are hungry for God and naturally create paths to him that make sense in their own minds, rather than submitting to the way that God has already provided through Jesus Christ. Bowing before the Lord in obedience and coming to him his way takes humility. And humility grinds the gears of human nature.

We are fascinated by our own thoughts. We are enamored with our own spiritual ideas that seem, at times, to make more sense than God's. We think God should be rational, in the human sense of the term. And so we use kindly human logic to make inane statements—*If God loves me, he wouldn't put this kind of restriction on me;* or *God could never send anyone to hell for eternity based on sins that were limited to a finite period of time;* or *This experience right now feels so good, it must be of God.* Such statements find no basis in the revealed Word of God yet are held with great conviction because of the way they fit comfortably into the human mind.

The problem with this comfort-based line of thinking and feeling is that God does a lot of things that we would never think of. Human thinking could never have invented God's plan of salvation. We would have created a gospel with far more human dignity and far less blood. We would have designed a religious system that doesn't take the subtle sins of the heart into account. You see, God does things and often asks things of us that make us uneasy. Listening to and obeying God will often make us uncomfortable. And we don't enjoy feeling uncomfortable.

Good or right feelings assure the human soul that it is doing the right thing before God, even when it is actually heading off in the wrong direction. I imagine Eve felt pretty good just before she ate the forbidden fruit. I wouldn't be surprised if Abraham felt fairly content just before he climbed into bed with Hagar. And King Saul probably felt quite happy with himself when he generously spared the life of King Agag as well as the best sheep, goats and cattle from the Amalekite flocks.

But following hard after God involves so much more than good feelings. In fact, good feelings are typically the lowest priority in the divine paradigm. God's big idea of his chosen ones experiencing a cross before receiving a crown makes certain of that.

The way to God is always through Jesus Christ, and we need to alert ourselves to anything in our spiritual lives that has nothing to do with him. According to the inspired Word of God, the Creator of the universe has nothing to give us beyond Christ (Hebrews 1:1–3).

We need to be very, very careful about the nature of our pursuit of God. Sincerity is not the key. Meaning well is not the key. Trying hard is not the key. The key to pursuing God properly is to do it only in such a fashion as he has revealed to us. As the prophet Zephaniah says, those who want to *"seek the Lord"* must *"follow his commands"* (see Zephaniah 2:3). The Psalmist says, *"Teach me your ways, O Lord, that I may live according to your truth"* (Psalm 86:11). He didn't say, *Help me out with my ways of pursuing you.*

I repeat myself. We must pay close attention to what God has revealed to us about this subject. No shortcuts. No alternate routes. Just the basics of the old, godly way that have never changed—intimate knowledge of the Scriptures, regular and honest communication with God, brokenness and humility of heart, full and ongoing repentance of sin, simple obedience to his revealed will, daily taking up a cross and dying to self, and letting Christ live his life through us by faith so that the fruit of the Spirit is manifested in our actions, causing us to have more hope and love and peace and joy and patience and goodness than is humanly or logically plausible.

Again, there are no shortcuts and no easier or better ways to a deeper knowledge of God than what he has shown us. All other paths are lies and their promoters charlatans.

Boxes

BACK TO THE GARDEN.

Obviously Eve was deceived by Satan. The serpent told her lies about God, and she believed him. She also felt inclined to degrade the importance of doing things according to God's specific instructions. With a few words outside of God's parameters, Eve was convinced—*"God knows that your eyes will be opened as soon as you eat it, and you will be like God, knowing both good and evil"* (Genesis 3:5). On the surface, this appeared to be a noble desire. What higher calling could exist for a creature formed in the image of the Almighty? After all, don't the Scriptures support this endeavor—to be just like God? *"You must be holy because I am holy"* (1 Peter 1:16). *"Imitate God"* (Ephesians 5:1).

The problem was not with Eve's desire. The problem was that she pursued that desire outside of the box that God had placed her in.

Boxes can be uncomfortable things.

People often say, *Don't put God in a box.* Such a statement supposedly liberates God to do whatever he pleases, because he is God. This phrase has a margin of truth to it but can also open us up to spiritual deception. When *letting God out of his box,* we must be careful not to assume that every event or thought that comes our way is necessarily safe. We want to be open to let God move as he pleases in people's lives but still be cautious about potential spiritual deception. Ultimately, we must remain focused on what he has already revealed to us about himself. We must, as the apostle Paul warned the church at Corinth, *"learn not to exceed what is written"* (1 Corinthians 4:6, NASB).

While we could never keep God in a box even if we tried, there is a far more significant issue at stake here regarding boxes. Instead of focusing on releasing God from the box we have supposedly put him in, we should be far more preoccupied with staying in the boxes where God has put us. We tend to want to climb out.

Quite often God puts his people in boxes and asks them to stay put. The menu in the Garden of Eden was such a box. For their own good and their own safety, God put a restriction on their behavior— do not eat from the tree of the knowledge of good and evil. The first couple had plenty of delicious options. But the one limitation prompted Eve to hop out of the box.

The temptation to leave the box will always be motivated by generous human logic. According to human calculation, it will feel right to disregard what God has said and pursue an alternative route. Certainly Eve must have convinced herself that her act of eating the fruit was a way of drawing closer to God.

But drawing closer to God in unsanctioned manners can be dangerous. Just ask any Israelite who ever tried to enter the wrong section of the tabernacle or the temple. The design of these holy structures could be likened to a series of boxes. The average Jewish citizen was to stay in the box of the outer court. The priests were allowed into a box of higher privilege and responsibility, the holy place. And the high priest, once a year, was permitted to enter the most exclusive box of all—the holy of holies—to make annual atonement for the sins of the people.

In Old Testament times, if an average Jewish citizen had spent enough time thinking about the topic, he might have come to the logical conclusion, *How silly that God would not want me to be near him.* If that same person then proceeded to leave his box and go into the holy of holies, he might have been struck dead.

So you have the ultimate presence of God just beyond that curtain. Kindly human logic asks why God would restrict a sincere seeker from entering his presence. Reasonable human thought might even judge God's behavior as unfair, to treat his earnest followers so harshly. Of course, the truth of the matter is this: such *reasonable* human thinking is rooted in too high a view of self and too low a view of God. We constantly struggle to grasp his utmost holiness and transcendence.

For reasons we do not always comprehend, God creates boxes and asks his followers to dwell securely and contently in them. The Ten Commandments could be considered such a box. The Decalogue was an enclosure of moral restrictions that was to guide the lives of Yahweh's chosen people so they would be a light of holiness to the other nations.

If an ancient Jew wanted to walk uprightly before God, there was no mystery involved in the process, no enigmatic or secret source of holiness. He or she was simply to do what God had revealed in the Law. *Stay in the box!*

Today, marriage could be considered a box that God has ordained for couples who want to live in sexual union. In times of relational hardship or boredom, it's easy to focus on the negativity of the box, the restrictions or boundaries it places on one's behavior. But when husbands and wives play their roles properly, the physical and emotional safety found within the marital box far outweighs the negative consequences associated with jumping out of it.

Even sincere people pursuing God will be tempted to jump out of divine boxes. The writer of

Ecclesiastes describes a box for honest seekers who want to enter into the presence of God properly. He says,

> *As you enter the house of God, keep your ears open and your mouth shut. It is evil to make mindless offerings to God. Don't make rash promises, and don't be hasty in bringing matters before God. After all, God is in heaven, and you are here on earth. So let your words be few.* (Ecclesiastes 5:1–2)

Countering our tendency to speak before we think, God wants us to use our words sparingly as we come into his presence. Our church box needs to be characterized more by listening than by talking. The implication then for our sanctification is that we need to hear what God has to say far more than he needs to be listening to what we have to say.

Furthermore, all instructions for holy living as outlined in the New Testament and modeled by Christ should be considered God's ordained boxes for our sacred containment. These guiding principles and rules have been established by him for our good. We cannot go wrong by following them. However, we get into trouble if we seditiously disregard them or hunt for alternative foundations of holiness apart from Christ.

Some things are clear. Do not limit God. Do not doubt what he can do in order to fulfill his divine purposes. But be careful not to travel paths that God has not ordained.

When we try to go places that God has not sanctioned, we can end up in strange locations in the name of greater holiness—*holy* laughter, barking like a dog, uncontrolled spasms and shaking—behaviors that have no foundation in God's revealed Word nor any useful role in conforming us to the image of Jesus Christ.

Again, this is not about *putting God in a box*—it's about staying in the boxes that he has put us in. This is the best approach because he is God and he's in charge. It's also good to remember that within these boxes he will fulfill his purposes for our lives. And it's also there that we will find peace and be eternally safe.

Collaboration

MANY HANDS MAKE LIGHT WORK.

This ancient proverb is mostly true. But sometimes many hands make the unsupervised work go too quickly and carelessly, causing mistakes and oversights. And sometimes too many cooks spoil the soup. Just assembling more humans together for a task does not absolutely guarantee a better product. There can be strength in numbers, but there can also be stupidity.

There is a natural human inclination to assume that more is better—more collaboration, more discussion, more people involved in the decision-making process. That is why much of the world is in love with democracy, the rule of many. Democracy feels better than dictatorship because of the freedoms we associate with this Athenian style of governance. But if, as Alexis de Tocqueville said, democracy is the tyranny of the majority, and the majority are idiots, then we're going to have some problems.

Humans merely consulting with each other is the source of a lot of problems in the pursuit of God. Religious discussions without a focus on Christ and the Scriptures often end up going in circles. Hours of Bible study where people just share their own ideas about the topic of the day can produce some poor understanding of what it means to develop a deep relationship with God. No matter how much human collaboration takes place, failing to bring God and the authority of his revealed Word into the equation can lead to erroneous theological conclusions and harmful outcomes.

Consider again some of the biblical stories we touched on earlier. Genesis 3 says that Eve took some of the fruit and ate it; *"Then she gave some to her husband, who was with her, and he ate it, too"* (3:6). There was no conversation with God, just two humans agreeing on a *good idea* that turned out to be bad. And as Eve passed the fruit on to Adam, he also sinned, causing sin to enter the entire world (Romans 5:12). Really bad idea!

The story of the Tower of Babel involved the same error—humans chatting it up together without consulting God.

> *They began saying to each other, "Let's make bricks and harden them with fire."…Then they said, "Come, let's build a great city for ourselves with a tower that reaches into the sky. This will make us famous and keep us from*

being scattered all over the world." (Genesis 11:3–4)

That committee meeting of a bunch of aggressive Type As resulted in more humiliation and confusion than fame.

In the saga of the Jewish patriarchs, when Joseph's siblings saw their little dreamer brother coming on the horizon, *"They made plans to kill him"* (Genesis 37:18). Another ill-advised board meeting without God at the table.

In the story of the golden calf, the Israelites *"gathered around Aaron"* (Exodus 32:1) and held a quick roundtable to decide what to do now that Moses had seemed to disappear from the scene. While considering the next steps for their future, there were no attempts to speak with God. There was no effort to reflect on what they knew to be true from previous revelations from their divine deliverer (e.g., Yahweh can bring really nasty plagues on his enemies and cause seawater to stand up when necessary). In their collective human wisdom, they built a ridiculous idol and proclaimed that the golden statue formed by their hands had pulled off all the great miracles of their recent history.

It's obvious—humans passing on ideas to one another without incorporating God into the dialogue often leads to erroneous outcomes. The Lord condemned the false prophets in Jeremiah's day for excluding him from their sermon preparation—

"I am against these prophets who steal messages from each other and claim they are from me" (Jeremiah 23:30).

Human teamwork without God's input leads to disastrous choices. The collaboration of the religious leaders of Jesus' day led to plans that resulted in the murder of their Messiah, the very Chosen One they had long anticipated.

People in religious authority are never exempt from bad decisions when God's revealed Word is ignored. After a benevolent discussion amongst the believers of the Corinthian church, their leadership came to the conclusion that they were okay with one of their upstanding members sleeping with his stepmom. After their congregational meeting with God in absentia, the Corinthian Christians probably felt like they were doing the right thing—being extra merciful, gracious, tolerant and kind.

The most potent result of humans sharing or passing on theological ideas without God or his Word in the picture is the faulty confidence it produces. Human collaboration tends to reassure people that they are on the right path. Naturally, we feel good when other people agree with us. We think we are doing it right because there are others on the team moving in the same direction.

It would be easy to misunderstand what I am saying here. I am not against collaboration and cooperation in decision-making. But in the realm of spiritual matters, life is more complex than deciding where to move the baptismal tank to or picking which division of the company gets the most development dollars in next year's budget.

In our passionate hunt for a meaningful relationship with God, we need God himself present in the discussion, not just the opinion of the pastor. We need to know what is written in the Bible, in all its entirety. We cannot simply rely on men and women putting their heads together to come up with some inspirational ideas. Without a serious attempt to invite God and Godlike thinking into the mix, we can easily be deceived and led into places that have little to do with an intimate knowledge of God.

Unfortunately, some contemporary religious movements are immersed in this collective *passing on* theme. In the Prophetic Movement and Word of Faith organizations, for example, spiritual power and authority are often referred to as a *blessing* or an *anointing* that one particular minister or prophet possesses. This power to do the work of God is supposedly passed on from one person to another. Religious leaders in these movements will refer to their own ministry as having been initiated by traveling to a particular location where this anointing or blessing was then passed on to them from another colleague.

On the surface, this *passing on* practice appears to have a biblical basis. The apostle Paul referred to his protégé, Timothy, receiving a spiritual gift when the elders of his church laid hands on him earlier in his life (1 Timothy 4:14). But any similarities between Timothy's experience and the practices of to-day's neo-charismatic movement are negligible. Timothy was under the care of the elders of his church and subject to scriptural teaching from infancy (2 Timothy 3:15). He did not run off to another locale to find a great work of the Spirit that he could absorb. And, unlike Word of Faith or Prophetic Movement congregations that focus heavily on health and wealth, spectacular visions and transportations to heaven, bizarre miraculous manifestations and wild circus-like theatre, Timothy's spiritual life was focused on reading Scripture, working hard for the Kingdom and living a life of personal holiness as an example to other believers (1 Timothy 4:6–16).

As in all things, the important principle is focus. Is the quest for God's power and presence human-oriented, or is it God-centered? Does the escalation in *spirituality* magnify people or glorify God? When someone says, *You must go to this or that city and attend the services of brother so-and-so because God is really moving there,* a caution light should go on. Proceed with care. Check it out if you must. Examine where the source of authority lies in the movement. Is it with the charismatic leader, or is it with a humble submission to the Scriptures?

Sacred sedition is often a part of movements characterized more by self-aggrandizement than biblical orthodoxy. God-vacant human collaboration in spiritual matters reeks of pride and often leads to the glorification of man. And any time creation is revered over the Creator, the mind gets messed up—

> *Yes, they knew God, but they wouldn't worship him as God or even give him thanks. And they began to think up foolish ideas of what God was like. As a result, their minds became dark and confused.* (Romans 1:21)

Spiritual deception is more likely to emerge when we are preoccupied with passing things on from person to person as opposed to seriously connecting with God through his Word.

New

PEOPLE RESPOND DIFFERENTLY WHEN THEY ARE warned about pursuing God outside the constraints of his revealed Word. The most common comeback is that *God is doing a new thing among his people.* The argument states that not all of God's work is recorded in the Bible. So, we as his children should feel free to pursue the Almighty in all manners possible, even those not specifically suggested by the Scriptures.

After all, doesn't the Word of God make reference to the Lord doing *new things* in terms of bringing revival to his people? *"Sing a new song to the Lord! Sing his praises from the ends of the earth!"* (Isaiah 42:10).

Isaiah is the most quoted of the prophets when this topic is up for discussion. *"For I am about to do something new. See, I have already begun! Do you not see it? I will make a pathway through the wilderness. I will create rivers in the dry wasteland"* (Isaiah 43:19).

Jeremiah concurred. *"For the Lord will cause something new to happen—Israel will embrace her God"* (Jeremiah 31:22).

> *"But this is the new covenant I will make with the people of Israel on that day," says the Lord. "I will put my instructions deep within them, and I will write them on their hearts. I will be their God, and they will be my people."* (Jeremiah 31:33)

Ezekiel too spoke of future revivals containing new elements for the people of God. *"And I will give them singleness of heart and put a new spirit within them. I will take away their stony, stubborn heart and give them a tender, responsive heart"* (Ezekiel 11:19).

Even the Messiah mentioned the theme of religious newness during his earthly ministry. When he spoke with the Pharisees about the conflict between his radical teaching and the traditional religious practice of first century Judea, he explained that when God does a new work, it cannot be blended in with the old comfortable forms of religion.

> *Besides, who would patch old clothing with new cloth? For the new patch would shrink and rip away from the old cloth, leaving an even bigger tear than before. And no one puts new wine into old wineskins. For the old skins would burst from the pressure, spilling the wine and ruining*

the skins. New wine is stored in new wineskins so that both are preserved. (Matthew 9:16–17)

Furthermore, the apostle Paul summed up the Christian life as an experience of complete renewal. *"This means that anyone who belongs to Christ has become a new person. The old life is gone; a new life has begun!"* (2 Corinthians 5:17).

Yes, it's absolutely essential to focus on the newness of life in Christ—the new birth, the new heart, the new man, the new covenant, the new Jerusalem, the new heaven and the new earth. The words of the Lord as recorded near the end of the New Testament back up this preoccupation. *"And the one sitting on the throne said, 'Look, I am making everything new!'"* (Revelation 21:5).

But to keep things in proper perspective, this principle of *newness* within the work of God must be explained more holistically.

Let's pull back so we can see the big picture.

God the Father commissioned Jesus to execute a salvation story that would buy back all of creation from the clutches of sin. Obviously, the divine plan would need to be radical. It involved waging war against the powers of the devil and the depravity of worldliness. But in the progress of God's redemptive revelation to mankind, divine truth is unveiled one step at a time. Things change. New practices emerge.

Consider the atoning power of blood, for instance. In the Garden of Eden, animal blood was shed for the sin of the first couple. Later, under the Mosaic covenant, blood sacrifice was expanded and ritualized with a formal system of priesthood managed by the descendants of Aaron. However, when Christ was crucified on the cross, the spotless Lamb of God became the final sacrifice that covered the sins of all time, thus ending the need for further blood sacrifices.

Consider also the primary targets of salvation in God's plan. At first he worked in the consciences of individual hearts. Then he chose the Jewish nation as a special people, consecrated for holiness and for the delivery of the promised Messiah. Now, in the fullness of Christ, God has expanded the offer of salvation freely to all the nations of the world (i.e., the Gentiles).

The specific details of God's expectations for his followers have changed over time. New ways of doing things were introduced in God's providential timing, but they never contradicted what was revealed in the past. God's new undertakings are always an extension of his original ideas, an historical outworking of his long-determined plans.

Because God doesn't change. *"I am the Lord, and I do not change"* (Malachi 3:6).

I often hear Christians saying that God is *doing a new thing* in their church. By this phrase, they usually mean that God has initiated some form of revival, blessing, outpouring or visitation in their midst. Yet when this new thing dies out quickly, what do we make of it? Did God suddenly change his mind? Were the events that transpired a result of God moving or just a bunch of humans following their own imaginations?

Attributing God's providence to human actions is always dicey. Sometimes the supposed move of God towards something new is clearly just worldliness creeping into the church. For example, a denominational decision to change its position on homosexuality in the name of a new work of God is quite precarious.

God doesn't normally change his mind on things. Even when there are adjustments in expectations of acceptable behavior, such variances are often the result of the mercy of God being gracious towards the sinful hearts of mankind. Take divorce, for instance. When he was questioned about this controversial topic, Jesus explained, *"Moses permitted divorce only as a concession to your hard hearts, but it was not what God had originally intended"* (Matthew 19:8).

God's ideas and intentions go way back. According to Ephesians 1, before the foundation of the world God had plans to adopt many followers as his own children, forgiving their sins and filling them with all good things through the power of Christ and the indwelling presence of the Holy Spirit.

Sometimes along the journey of God's unfolding plan, he makes changes because of the human responses involved in the story. For example, there was a time in Jewish history when God chose the city of Shiloh as the place to meet with his people. There, in the heart of today's West Bank, the tabernacle stayed for over three hundred years, making it the center of Jewish religious activity. But then, because of the wickedness of the priests and some poor decision-making on the part of the children of Israel, Shiloh was abandoned as a sacred location. In time, Jerusalem was established as the new place where God would meet with his people.

In this case, it's fair to say that God did something new, but it was not really that new at all. God has always had a plan to fellowship with his creation. He continually desires to meet with his people and bless them as they walk in obedience. Just because the venue for his desire changes, the intentions don't.

This is similar to what often happens with family vacation plans. You have it all calculated perfectly at the beginning—travel routes are determined, hotels are booked and specific activities anticipated. But as life happens, alterations to the specific details occur. Small logistics are changed and divergent trails are incorporated into the overall design. Now, the master plan doesn't change—you still get the family to Disney World—but the trip ends up looking a little different.

There are no mysteries in God's big idea for the universe. Since the Fall of mankind, our Heavenly Father has been working towards the reconciliation of all creation back to himself through the sacrificial blood of his Son Jesus Christ. Even though there appears to be deviating subplots developing because of sinful human behavior, the big overall plot is firmly fixed, gently guided by the sovereign hand of the omniscient and omnipotent Creator.

From the beginning, God has always told us what we need to know.

The Lord our God has secrets known to no one. We are not accountable for them, but we and our children are accountable forever for all that he has revealed to us, so that we may obey all the terms of these instructions. (Deuteronomy 29:29)

The New Testament reiterates the fact that there are no mysterious resources for pursuing God. He has already provided all we need.

By his divine power, God has given us everything we need for living a godly life. We have received all of this by coming to know him, the one who called us to himself by means of his marvelous glory and excellence. (2 Peter 1:3)

Notice, the Christian receives all that is needed by coming to know God. And the best way to know God is to get to know what he has already said about himself in his Word.

Quite often, people are quick to announce the arrival of a new work of God in the church. But such claims typically sound very territorial by nature. They say God is strongly moving in this or that particular place. The implication, then, is that if others want to be a part of this new work of God, they need to go to that specific location in order to partake of it. My initial response to such a claim would be that when God is doing something new in his well-established plans of old, it's probably happening in more than just one place.

The term *revival* is used somewhat loosely these days. When people lay claim to a powerful new work of God in their midst, they call it a revival. However, more often than not, this revival is focused far more on demonstrative displays of signs and wonders accompanied by great feelings of love and power as opposed to a wide scale movement of brokenness and confession of personal sin (the marks of a true revival). And truth be told, many of the manifestations present in the most recent so-called revivals (laughter, jerking, slaying, animals noises) are not new at all—they have been part of Hinduism, other Eastern religions and kundalini cults for thousands of years.[1]

---

1 "Shocking Footage: False Spirits Invade the Church," YouTube video, posted by "JohnTheBaptistTV" on June 26, 2010, http://www.youtube.com/watch?feature=player_embedded&v=-RVAu1uGkew

In fact, many of the well-known revivalists of the past (John Wesley, George Whitefield, Jonathan Edwards, Charles Finney), though calling for repentance with great fervor, saw the fringe emotional excesses of their meetings as a sign of demonic counterfeit invasion.[2] John Wesley warned his listeners,

> *Do not hastily ascribe things to God. Do not easily suppose dreams, voices, impressions, visions, or revelations to be from God. They may be from Him. They may be from Nature. They may be from the devil. Therefore believe not every spirit, but 'try the spirits whether they be from God.'*[3]

Authors Jessie Penn-Lewis and Evan Roberts wrote War On The Saints: A Disclosure Of The Deceptive Strategies Used By Evil Spirits Against God's People *to combat the deception that arose during the Welsh revival that occurred at the turn of this century. Both were very involved with the revival and were extremely*

---

2 "Slain in What Spirit, Part 1," InPlainSite.org, accessed May 4, 2013, http://www.inplainsite.org/html/slain_in_the_spirit_1.html

3 "The Contemporary Church: Slain in the Spirit," InPlainSite.org, accessed May 4, 2013, http://www.inplainsite.org/html/slain_in_the_spirit_1.html

*concerned about the demonic manifestations
that began to dominate their meetings.*[4]

Besides, revival is not primarily about God doing something spectacular that he has never done
before. Spiritual revival is, in fact, a new discovery
of an old truth. To help us understand this, think
of the work of EMS personnel reviving someone
in cardiac arrest. When they *revive* the person, they
are not giving them new life, they are restoring the
life that they used to have. God has never created a
new message that is different from his original intentions. The ministries of Elijah, John the Baptist and
the apostle Paul, for example, involved fresh experiences and deeper teachings, but their messages presented more of a restoration or fulfillment of God's
original plans than a formulation of something entirely different.

Revivals always involve a reawakening of original truths that God has already given to his children.
When the Jewish prophets spoke of a time of revival
when God would write his law on his people's hearts,
it was *his* law that was being written there, not something new or different. Historically, true revivals
involved genuine life transformation and sweeping

social change. As masses of people renewed their commitments to Christ and his claims on their lives, the message of the gospel became famous and there was a renewed interest in the truths of God. In more recent revivals, such as the one in China, increased spiritual fervor has also been accompanied by increased persecution (2 Timothy 3:12).

Today, many who claim to be experiencing a new work of revival in their midst are not demonstrating greater holiness or a deeper knowledge of God. There may be a lot of noise, many references to the riches and health of the Prosperity Gospel and regular displays of supernatural power, but very little personal repentance. This contradicts the teaching of James, who describes the process of drawing near to God as involving more weeping and mourning than laughter (James 4:8–10).

In the time period leading up to the Jewish captivity carried out by the Babylonian king, Nebuchadnezzar, the chosen people were walking in wickedness on many levels. They thought they were okay because they still had the temple in their midst. But God called for a whole-scale repentance to avert their impending judgment. And he referred to this revival as a return to the old, godly way. Listen to Jeremiah 6:16. You can hear the heart cry of God: *"Stop at the crossroads and look around. Ask for the old, godly way, and walk in it. Travel its path, and you will find rest for your souls. But you reply, 'No, that's not the road we want!'"*

The notion of *old* is not typically attractive today. In our postmodern culture, it carries the connotation of withered and useless, devoid of any true value. But in the mind of God, *old* means eternal, everlasting and timeless. Civilizations rise and fall, ideas come and go, *"but the word of our God stands forever"* (Isaiah 40:8). And the Word of God preaches a cross before a crown. People don't want to travel that path. They don't want to traverse the age-old trail of being broken before God and humbly submitting to his righteous conviction of sin in order to pursue him more deeply. They do, however, feel a strong attraction to something that feels new spiritually, something that is less demanding morally, and a movement that is accompanied by good feelings and a vague love for God.

The concepts of salvation and consecration that were formed in the mind of God before the foundation of the world have never changed. In some respects, that's why it's tough to say that there is anything truly new in terms of seeking God. Perhaps that is what the author of Ecclesiastes was getting at when he said, *"History merely repeats itself. It has all been done before. Nothing under the sun is truly new. Sometimes people say, 'Here is something new!' But actually it is old; nothing is ever truly new"* (Ecclesiastes 1:9–10).

We do not have a natural affinity for the old, godly way. We do, however, have a hankering for something that seems new and exciting.

As we engage in our quest for a deeper relationship with God, we must be aware of the pitfall of sacred sedition that can ironically sidetrack us from our goal. It is easy to be enticed by shortcuts, mystery paths or new-fangled movements that have the flavor and feel of true revival but lack its long-lasting impact and commitment to the old, godly way of personal holiness.

Authority

THIS CHAPTER IS PERHAPS THE MOST IMPORTANT ONE because the practice of pursuing God rightly is firmly based on the issue of authority. Who has the right to say how I should pursue God? Who do I listen to? Why can't I do what I think seems reasonable? Are there many different paths to the same destination? Surely my heart can tell me when God is doing something special in my soul.

It can be overwhelming to grasp the concept of connecting meaningfully with a deity who created our boundless universe. Astronomers now estimate it to be at least 46.6 billion light years across.[5] Truthfully, as a measly human on this third rock from the sun, is it possible to attain a personal relationship

---

5 Paul Halpern, Edge of the Universe (Hoboken, NJ: John Wiley and Sons, 2012), 10

with the God who holds a gazillion atoms of creation together by his phenomenal power?

For such a tremendous endeavor—intimate and genuine interpersonal contact with God—there must be an authoritative path to keep us from going all over the map. If solving this conundrum of establishing a spiritual link with God were left up to us mere mortals, we would be lost. Sure, human imagination creates soup kitchens and indigent hospitals, but it also creates Nazism and bestiality porn sites. Human resourcefulness by itself cannot take us to God. We're too frail and fickle.

The one who made everything also makes the rules. The Creator himself would have to be the one who establishes the route to find him. There must be a divine authority on this matter. Good news— there is. The very God who made everything also made a definitive way for us to connect with him. I know it sounds unglamorous and very old school, but this authority is the Bible.

Unfortunately, the Bible does not automatically command the attention it used to. Now that civilization is postmodern and sophisticated, people want something more hip, more chic, more in tune with their feelings and personal experiences. Atheistic philosophies are fabricated in an attempt to meet the needs of the human soul apart from the Word of God.

Existentialism, for example, has established the paradigm of personal truth—people create their own truth by what is meaningful to them. It's alluring because it feels warm and fuzzy, and it gels with the uncertainty and general angst of the twenty-first century.

Existentialism is attractive but wrong. If there is nothing that is absolutely true, there is nothing for us to do...about anything. There is no meaning in life, because everything is relative. Good and evil are determined by personal choices. You can help the old lady cross the street or you can run her down with your car. Both choices have equal worth. There is no purpose in life, because there is nothing that is unequivocally right or wrong. We live. We die. So what? You love me. I kill you. Whatever. When we abandon the premise of an absolute authority, we introduce ourselves to all sorts of nonsense.

This is how I see it: I am fearfully and wonderfully made. Just the complexity of protein delivery in the cells of my body is enough to convince me of this. I am not here by accident. I don't continue to exist by chance. There is a sovereign God who cares enough about me to keep my heart beating. There is a divine being who gives me every breath I breathe. That kind of all-powerful dominion commands authority. And his authoritative instructions for life, liberty and the pursuit of holiness are unfolded within the pages of his Word, the Bible.

When we declare ourselves to be pursuers of God, there will be fellow travelers who want to share their stories with us. As we listen to what they have to say, we cannot assume that everything we hear is absolutely true. We must hold up their narratives to the light of the Scriptures. And even when people back up their experiences with a single proof text, we need to scrutinize their accounts according to the entirety of God's Word. There must be an outright authority to which we can anchor our thoughts and experiences. Otherwise, we are adrift in an ocean of intellectual, spiritual and emotional speculation.

Now, if you have not grown up in a Christian home and your religious perspective is a little broader than mine, you might be thinking a bit more cosmopolitan at this point. What about other religions? Don't they have authoritative writings as well? Don't they tell of other pathways to a meaningful union with God?

Yes and no.

The revered writings of world religions do speak of different gods and various sacred practices for proper living, but they lack the efficacious authority of the Christian Bible. World religions always involve the story of fairly decent people reaching up to a deity or deities, striving to gain salvation through virtuous human effort alone.

Christianity, on the other hand, is about God graciously stooping down to rescue a sinful, needy humanity through the work of his Son, Jesus Christ. In that sense, Christianity stands clearly apart from other world religions. World religions are concerned with upholding the dignity of humans. Christianity has a plan to save only those who recognize their own sinfulness. World religions have self-generated good deeds. Christianity has an imparted new life in Christ. World religions have good men. Christianity has the God-man.

I know it sounds arrogant. How can one confidently assert that the Bible is right and all other religious writings are wrong? I cannot do justice to this topic in a few paragraphs. Entire libraries and seminary courses have been created on the topic of scriptural apologetics (i.e., how we know the Bible is the only true spiritual authority). And yet, even after fully immersing oneself in the theological study of the authority of the Bible, faith is still required to accept it as God's Word.

There are all sorts of great reasons why the Bible can be seen as unique and miraculously inspired by God—the number of different authors, the lengthy time over which it was written, its utterly unparalleled ancient manuscript support, its bizarre diversity and unity. If you were an odds-maker, based on all available evidence, the best bet for the right spiritual answers would be the Bible over the writings of other world religions. But none of these things matter if a skeptic chooses to not believe. As I said, a full measure of faith is still required.

In fact, even Christians who believe in the general authority of the Bible must exercise faith in the Scriptures when the going gets rough. When the Bible says tough things that go against what we want to hear, we must proceed with the simple faith of a child, and obey. If the Bible *is* the one true authority, then it is the one true authority. We can't just make it our authority when we feel like it or when it seems to fit in with benevolent human logic or when it resonates with our own experiences. The Bible is either theologically right or it's not. I am assuming it's right—all of it.

And if the Bible is the only thing that we know for sure to be absolutely right, it must be the standard by which we scrutinize all extra-biblical revelations, prophecies and teachings about getting to know God.

Yet as much as we may believe this to be true, we are inclined to wander. It's tempting to go beyond what God has said. God reveals his Word to us, but we want something more, something different. The book of Jeremiah illustrates this human tendency. On more than one occasion in this prophetic book, God delivered his message of judgment upon the Jewish people through his true prophet Jeremiah while false prophets promised everything would be okay. The Jewish kings were repeatedly attracted to the good news, so they didn't particularly like Jeremiah or his message. He always sounded too pessimistic.

In Jeremiah 37, the prophet delivered a message of destruction to King Zedekiah that was not well received. Here's what happened. The Jews were being besieged by the Babylonians. But the Babylonians took off when Pharaoh Hophra's armies from Egypt arrived to help out. Zedekiah assumed they were now safe, but Jeremiah had a word from the Lord for the king: *"Pharaoh's army is about to return to Egypt, though he came here to help you. Then the Babylonians will come back and capture this city and burn it to the ground"* (Jeremiah 37:7–8).

Jeremiah clearly stated what the Lord had to say about the matter. As usual, God's authoritative Word was greeted with hostility by those in human authority. The Jerusalem city officials flogged the poor prophet and threw him in a dungeon. Later on, Zedekiah secretly brought Jeremiah back to the palace, where he again asked him, *"Do you have any messages from the Lord?"* (Jeremiah 37:17). Uh, yah. Duh. The same one I gave you before—*"you will be destroyed by the King of Babylon"* (37:17)…which, for the record, did happen. How typical. We hear or read what God has said and yet we ask, *Has he said anything else?*

We always want to go around or beyond what God says. *I don't like that message. Is there another one?*

It shouldn't surprise us. Satan did the same thing. Instead of staying within his prescribed position declared by the Word of the Lord, he said, *"I will ascend to heaven and set my throne above God's stars"* (Isaiah 14:13). I will go beyond what God has declared. I will do my own thing. And satanic spirits can urge sincere believers to do the same thing, to go beyond God's parameters and his declared Word.

The writer of Psalm 119 establishes a strong connection between energetically seeking God and obeying his Word: *"Joyful are people of integrity, who follow the instructions of the Lord. Joyful are those who obey his laws and search for him with all their hearts"* (Psalm 119:1–2). Earnest but naïve believers can be lured to chase strange doctrines and practices in their pursuit of God because they have failed to keep themselves tethered to the Scriptures. The energy and excitement are attractive. The music is stirring to their souls. The miraculous signs and wonders are convincing (Matthew 24:24). Feels so good, can't be wrong!

Or can it?

Ironically, the temptation to wander beyond the boundaries of Scripture can come from a cursory knowledge of it. We have all we need in the Bible. But people don't know the Word of God. They don't read it enough on their own. They don't study it regularly. They don't meditate on it or pray over its precepts. They don't repeatedly invite the Holy Spirit to apply it to their lives. They stick to the parts they like (Psalms, Proverbs and the New Testament) and avoid the parts they don't (much of the Old Testament).

And because many believers don't know their Bible fully, their relationship with the Lord is dry. And because their relationship is dry, they thirst for some form of revival. But the revival they crave is not a biblical revival, one that entails repentance of sin, deep humility before God and obedience to his commands. No, they just want a quick fix, a drug to cheer them up. Instead of learning to bear a cross for the cause of Christ, they want a rush, a simple high that immediately elevates them into the esoteric realm of God's love and power.

Spiritual dearth can come from a Scriptural famine. There is a deficiency, and remedial shortcuts seem tempting. It's easy to neglect the work that needs to be done to become properly familiar with the Scriptures. Godliness requires training (1 Timothy 4:7), and those who fail to train end up spiritually dull and baby-like (Hebrews 5:11–14). If our spiritual feasting on the Word of God is limited to Sunday morning sermons, we will not be able to draw close to God, not in any sustainable fashion.

And yet we cannot view God's Word simply as a massive textbook that needs to be mastered for the final exam. And it is far more than just an answer key to check for the solutions on a religious test. The Bible is unlike any other book. It's divinely inspired. It's living and potent.

For the word of God is alive and powerful. It is sharper than the sharpest two-edged sword, cutting between soul and spirit, between joint and marrow. It exposes our innermost thoughts and desires. (Hebrews 4:12)

The Bible is the very breath of God. To inhale it is to inhale him. But like breath, the inhalation must be constant to survive.

And the more we are humbly immersed in its pages in genuine spiritual hunger, the more real God's Word becomes in our hearts. As we learn to submit to its directives for our lives, God's presence grows more tangible. And his voice becomes more audible.

The true way to God is hard. In fact, friendship with God is only possible because of the immense suffering of Christ (Romans 5:10). And true Christian character develops when we learn to endure problems and trials (Romans 5:3–4). If we think we are following God and our lives are chugging along quite smoothly, we may want to check the map. For Christ made it very clear that there is a high cost involved in being his disciple on the road to heaven—people who hurt us deeply must be forgiven, all love must be unselfish, holiness takes precedence over happiness, sacrifice trumps self-service and the Kingdom of God is more important than my big-screen TV.

Without the authoritative guidance of God's Word, we are vulnerable to enticing yet unproductive rabbit trails and deceptive allurements along our path to God. Without the confines of Scripture, we may discover our sacred intentions to actually be seditious rebellion. Instead of finding him in all his holiness, we may find ourselves distracted by all forms of silliness promoted by televangelists and fake faith-healers who have more secret sins and vacation homes than most Hollywood movie stars.

Deception

MANY PEOPLE WITH GOOD INTENTIONS AND SINCERE desires often end up missing the mark as they passionately pursue God. They want to be close to God, but they try to do it their own way instead of God's way. As discussed earlier, the Scriptures are replete with examples of people who thought they were following God, but because they did it in their own fashion, they ended up in places of sin and disobedience, far outside the will of God.

Just wanting to do the right thing in no way assures us of actually doing it. Our spiritual growth does not just happen. We do not mature in Christ without resisting evil forces. We need to be aware of those powers that are working against us as we endeavor to develop our relationship with God and grow in holiness.

It is shamefully naïve for us to ignore the reality of spiritual deception in our world. We cannot make an effort to draw near to God without attracting strong opposition from the spiritual realm. The devil and his cohorts of demons do not want us to get this right. That's why Jesus, when he taught us to pray, included the phrase *"Rescue us from the evil one"* (Matthew 6:13).

People living in the West have a negligible grasp of spiritual matters. Those outside the new life of Christ spend little or no time thinking about spiritual opposition. The universe, though apparently infinite, is viewed as a closed system with no divine forces at work. Natural causes account for all behaviors and events. Independent men and women supposedly create human destinies by their own wills. Any spiritual blips on the radar are casually brushed aside as unexplainable anomalies or the onions from last night's pizza.

For the worldly-minded masses of the West, reality consists of what is visible, and life entails the here and now. The spiritual forces of darkness like it that way. When people in our culture obliviously motor along with their careers, mortgage payments and family vacations, Satan's best plan of attack is to go unnoticed. When people are functioning void of a relationship with God, the devil does not want to make himself flamboyantly evident.

For people separated from God, demonic temptations largely take the form of life decisions and pleasurable activities that keep them busy and happy. Such people feel content that they are living a good life, doing all that is necessary to be considered a decent person. Non-Christians have no awareness of the law of sin and death within them and no attentiveness to their need to repent of that sin. And Satan musters every possible diversion in his power to keep lost souls from feeling the conviction of the Holy Spirit. For the unbeliever, spiritual deception predominantly takes the form of distraction (Matthew 13:7, 22).

For the saved, deception can also involve distraction, but it's far more elaborate. The devil also loves to wrap lies within truth. And he likes to toy with believers' sensitive searching hearts. People who want something badly enough often fail to discriminate how they are attaining their desires. Desperately hungry people will eat almost anything.

Discussions of evil spiritual forces often stir up debate regarding where such powers came from. This might seem like a strange place to talk about the origin of evil, but bear with me because it's important. To understand spiritual deception, one must recognize the source and nature of evil.

The questions have been posed time and time again by both skeptics and sincere seekers—*How could a good God create evil? And if he didn't actually create it, then why would an all-powerful God impotently allow its arrival and then tolerate its expansion throughout his creation?* Fair questions. Why is there evil in the world?

To comprehend the concepts of good and evil, it helps to parallel them to the principles of heat and cold as well as the nature of light and darkness. You see, cold and darkness do not actually exist; that is, they are not concrete entities in themselves. Cold is just the absence of heat. Darkness is the absence of light. Likewise, evil is the absence of good.

Now, even though heat and cold, light and darkness, and good and evil may seem to exist side by side, there is no question as to where the power lies. The second element always yields to the first. Cold immediately surrenders when heat is introduced into an environment. Darkness bows in submission when light is shone on its shadows. And evil is no match for good.

Again, evil is not an entity in itself; it is the absence of good, or God. Everything God is, thinks and does is good. Everything apart from God is evil. God did not create evil. He is not responsible for it. Created beings with free choice had the ability to stay within the realm of the good. Evil materialized as the commands of God were abandoned. Evil emerges wherever God is disregarded, just as darkness develops where light diminishes and a chill arrives as heat decreases. Even today, evil continues to arise wherever beings with free choice opt for independence over submission to God.

The battle between good and evil is not some eternal struggle like the yin-yang tension of Eastern religions. It has a lot more to do with our behavior—we simply need to learn to distinguish between the act of aligning with the Creator and the act of rebelling against him. When God is properly understood and pursued in truth, the outcome is ultimately good (remembering that *good* is not equal to feeble human notions of *nice* or *pleasant*). But when we act independently of God, our deeds, though seemingly good, eventually lead to some form of evil.

Keep in mind that this matter of good and evil is not like a brawl between equal forces, a couple of well-matched burly cowboys going at it in the saloon. Just as darkness cannot hold back the sunrise and cold cannot resist the introduction of heat, no evil intention or action can hold back the good work of God in history. Good will not just *eventually* win over evil; good is *already* and *always* winning as God builds his invisible Kingdom with the hearts, minds and wills of those children who surrender to him.

In the beginning, God created Satan as an angel with great authority, apparently the head of all spiritual beings. And God gave him a free will; he was not a subservient robot. When the devil chose to rebel against God, taking other angels with him, he established a network of evil in the heavenly realm. This system of spiritual opposition began to encourage other created beings to rebel against God, both blatantly and subtly. Our first witness to this Machiavellian ploy was in the Garden of Eden—*"Eve was deceived by the cunning ways of the serpent"* (2 Corinthians 11:3).

As discussed earlier, Satan's modus operandi in the Garden was to attract Eve with assurances of a closer connection with her Creator—*You'll be just like God, knowing good and evil.* The woman believed the lies because they promised to satisfy her hunger for a deeper relationship with God. But because the action of eating the fruit was based on fraud instead of truth, it led to the Fall. And ever since mankind's initiation into this mode of rebellion against God, Satan has continued with his goal—to *"deceive the nations"* (Revelation 20:3).

So, our enemy is powerful, but not all-powerful. He will one day be fully defeated. But for now, he continues his dance of deception. Because he poses as *"an angel of light"* (2 Corinthians 11:14), the devil's lures are enticing—that's why they're called lures. His scams have the appearance of truth but are part of a comprehensive evil scheme. He knows where he is headed because of his rebellion. And he's working hard to bring all of humanity to the same horrid destiny assigned to him.

Satan's work of spiritual deception is most evident in the presence of cults, world religions and perversions of Christianity. The devil's main plan of attack in opposing God is to promote not atheism but false religion. He does not want to prove the non-existence of God; he wants to usurp the Lord's authority and have human and spirit beings worship him instead.

Cults, world religions and perversions of Christianity project shimmering paths of superficial goodness but provide no real hope for the needs of a sinful humanity. Without the true message of the gospel proclaiming the death and the resurrection of our Savior, these false religions stumble around in the dark. Despite their errant nature, they continue to grow in popularity and maintain their look of suitable alternatives to pure Christianity. They seem genuine, viable and useful in a world that cherishes tolerance. They even promote decent human behavior such as devotion to peace (Buddhism), and encourage the development of noble character (Confucianism's Five Virtues).

But upon closer scrutiny, these false religions serve up a menu of horrid dishes that reveal the nature of their secret and silent sponsor. Only the devil could blend in such vile behavior amidst the pleasant ingredients of human kindness and devoted religious ritual. Only the devil could embroider such contemptible practice into the fabric of fine-looking religion—cruel treatment of women (fundamentalist Islamic practice and Hindu's tradition of Sati), nasty abuse of human rights in general (Hindu caste system), human sacrifice (Aztec religion), insane murderous campaigns (fundamentalist Islamic terrorism), duplicity and sexual abuse (cult leaders), mass suicide (Jim Jones) and cannibalism (animist tribes of South America and Southeast Asia).

Cults, world religions and perversions of Christianity attract people because they reinforce a sense of human confidence and independence. *I'm good enough to make it on my own. If there is a problem in me, I can fix it. I can even make the world a better place.* And yet, repeatedly, these satanic spiritual counterfeits fall short of their claims. They show they cannot fill the emptiness of the human soul, fix the selfish intentions of human nature or solve the social problems of the countries they dominate. In stark contrast to the deceptive darkness of false religion stands the luminescent brightness of the Son of God. Christ, as the light of the world, brings not only radiance to every shadowy path but satisfaction for every hunger and satiation for every thirst.

In contrast to the spiritually lost, genuine followers of Jesus Christ know the reality of the goodness of God through his Son. They understand their own natural darkness and they know why Christ died for them. They understand who they would be without Christ. But starting off on the right path does not guarantee a good ending to the story. Christians can be deceived by the devil as easily as non-Christians can.

Cults and world religions do not hold the exclusive rights to spiritual deception. It is also rampant within the Christian church. This subject will be explored in more depth in a later chapter. As we'll see, the trickery and fraud are part of a high stakes game of eternal destiny, and our enemy is a lot smarter than us.

The Bible says Satan is clever and cunning, with crafty strategies (Ephesians 6:11). He uses disguises to make himself more attractive. But all the while, *"He prowls around like a roaring lion, looking for someone to devour"* (1 Peter 5:8). Wanting more than just the death of genuine believers, Satan wants to cause them to fall away from the faith through disbelief or discouragement. He is also quite happy to see them slip into silly sidetracks that pretend to offer genuine spiritual growth but end up in further disillusionment.

Because the battle against the devil is so substantial, Christians must suit up appropriately to ensure the fight goes in their favor.

> *Put on all of God's armor so that you will be able to stand firm against all strategies of the devil. For we are not fighting against flesh-and-blood enemies, but against evil rulers and authorities of the unseen world, against mighty powers in this dark world, and against evil spirits in the heavenly places.* (Ephesians 6:11–12)

If we actually believe this, we should be concerned. Evil spirits want to take us out of the game. Things we cannot see want to cause us pain. It's freaky to think about the reality of demons entering into our life space to influence us. The prospect of Satan devising downfall strategies specifically for each of us is unnerving. If it doesn't frighten us, we're not taking it seriously enough.

And yet, this is not an unwinnable battle or one that we need to fight by ourselves. God wins it for us. The full instructions in Ephesians 6 break down the logistics for battle preparation when anticipating spiritual warfare—arming ourselves with the girdle of truth, the breastplate of righteousness, the gospel of peace, the shield of faith, the helmet of salvation and the sword of the Spirit.

The apostle Paul's teaching is very clear. Our enemy has plans for our defeat. If we don't clothe ourselves in Christ (another way of saying *the armor of God*), we are going down for the count. However, when we, by faith, put on every piece of God's armor, the promise is solid—we will be able to repel our enemy. *"Then after the battle you will still be standing firm"* (Ephesians 6:13).

But Satan and his emissaries of evil are not the only adversaries involved in our spiritual deception. Besides demonic forces fighting against us, the power of our own sin within us works contrary to our pursuit of God (James 1:14). Deeply rooted within human nature lies a contamination of selfishness more stubborn than the crabgrass in my front lawn.

Even without satanic suasion, we find ourselves pursuing all manners of evil when we do what comes naturally. Our sinful flesh is just as sneaky as the devil himself. Without proper monitoring, it can pop up and spoil even the finest intentions for godliness and a closer relationship with the Creator.

The apostle Paul referred to this evil bent within our wicked flesh as the *law of sin.* And this law of sin attacks us most aggressively when we are at our best. In Romans 7, Paul said he experienced the strongest spiritual opposition from within when he was trying to do the right thing. On the contrary, if we backslide, it's a very relaxed and casual process; there is no noise of spiritual opposition to thwart our drift.

But when we want to make things right in our relationship with God, when we want to learn to walk by faith in the power of Christ, our flesh invents every possible reason why not to go there. When we determine to do even the simplest task for God, sin fights us right at that point, making us drowsy when we should pray or stingy when we should give.

Amidst our desires to grow closer to God, we must not forget that our hearts are desperately wicked, deceitful above all things (Jeremiah 17:9). Jesus called the heart the fountain of sin (Matthew 15:19) and a treasure chest where we sock away evil (Luke 6:45). The sinful flesh within us is a nemesis that must be recognized and defeated if we are to dodge deception and grow spiritually.

Again, this is not a battle we undertake single-handedly. By faith, it is the Holy Spirit who wages war against our flesh. But if we are not cognizant of the need to battle, we will be deceived by ourselves and hampered in our journey to holiness.

And besides the trickery of the devil and the enticements of the flesh, we also need to be vigilant regarding the destructive power of worldliness. The operational system of this damaged planet is void of anything good. The principles that drive this fallen world are completely contrary to the concept of true spiritual growth or the advancement of the Kingdom of God. People who genuinely follow after God are referred to as being *"not of this world"* (John 18:36, KJV).

All the components of this worldly system—the lust of the eyes, the lust of the flesh and the boastful pride of life—are prepared to pounce, ready to trump the actions of even the most sincere believer's life. Unless we guard against it deliberately, worldliness can rear its ugly head, even in the midst of attempted godly pursuits. Intentions must be examined carefully and subtle sins exposed.

Even as I write this book, I must be aware of my motives. Is this endeavor truly about knowing God better, or about the fact that I know how to put words together on a page in a semi-interesting fashion? I need the power of Christ to safeguard me from my flesh and from worldliness. Regularly, I need to repent and redirect every avenue of my life so that it remains focused on God instead of my pride, my desire to have everything I see or my cravings for physical pleasure (1 John 2:16).

Malicious forces of demonic, worldly and selfish origins work against us knowing God better.

They resist our progress towards the Almighty and our growth in greater holiness. They deceive us about right and wrong. They offer a lot of wrong that looks a lot like right.

If we want to seek the Lord in truth and avoid derailment by deceptive lies, we need to learn to discern what is genuinely from God and what is not. We need to learn to discriminate between that which helps us pursue God and that which pretends to help but actually hinders.

Discernment

THE PSALMIST DAVID WROTE THE FOLLOWING LINES in one of his songs: *"The Lord is close to all who call on him, yes, to all who call on him in truth"* (Psalm 145:18). The paramount words in this verse are the last two. Their presence implies that there are ways to call upon the Lord falsely. Sincerity and effort are not the decisive variables. Truth is what matters.

If sincerity and effort were the only requirements, surely the 850 prophets of Baal and Asherah that took on Elijah at the Mount Carmel barbeque would have fared better. Almost a thousand religious men fervently cried out for divine intervention for the duration of an entire working day. Besides verbal raving, they even cut themselves in frenzied religious devotion to get their god to act and send fire from heaven.

From our perspective, we would say that these prophets were calling on a false deity, Baal instead of Yahweh. But that is not how they would have seen it. They would not have thought of themselves as false prophets. After all, who would devote their entire working career to a cause known to be bogus? No, they thought they were serving a true deity— Baal, the god of rain, thunder, fertility and agriculture. And they probably looked like regular, well-dressed religious guys. So the real issue at stake here was the struggle between truth and deception. Elijah called upon Yahweh in truth. His competition was deceived. In the spiritual realm, this is always the core issue.

As we discussed last chapter, spiritual deception can mess up our attempts to pursue God properly.

Christ told his disciples that, in the last days before his coming, there would be a rise of false prophets and false messiahs who would *"perform great signs and wonders so as to deceive, if possible, even God's chosen ones"* (Matthew 24:24). The apostle Paul had a similar cautionary warning for his younger protégé regarding the popularity of unsound doctrine in the future.

For a time is coming when people will no longer listen to sound and wholesome teaching. They will follow their own desires and will look for teachers who will tell them whatever their itching ears want to hear. They will reject the truth and chase after myths. (2 Timothy 4:3–4)

During his earthly ministry, Jesus addressed the issue of spiritual deception and the need for discernment. *"Beware of false prophets who come disguised as harmless sheep but are really vicious wolves. You can identify them by their fruit, that is, by the way they act"* (Matthew 7:15–16).

Christ cautioned people who showed interest in pursuing God—such an endeavor is not without confusion. Connecting with the Maker of everything is no casual or haphazard matter. Christ referred to the true way to God as narrow and the path to destruction as broad. He said few will survive the skinny path to heaven while many will end up trekking down the interstate to hell.

Christ also said many will try to enter the Kingdom of God but will fail. Many will also do kingdomesque activities but in the end will be shown to be fakers who don't actually know the King (Matthew 7:21–23). All people who call themselves Christians are not necessarily in the Kingdom. All words pouring out of Christian contexts are not necessarily true.

Hence the need for discernment, the ability to identify that which is genuinely from God and that which is counterfeit.

The apostle Paul likened the theologically deceived to juveniles who are vulnerable to a wild spiritual ride. He called for close attention to the teachings of Christ's true messengers so that there would be a proper maturing in Christ.

Then we will no longer be immature like children. We won't be tossed and blown about by every wind of new teaching. We will not be influenced when people try to trick us with lies so clever they sound like the truth. (Ephesians 4:14)

But Paul was not opposed to the concept of someone speaking in a prophetic mode. He told the Thessalonian church, *"Do not scoff at prophecies, but test everything that is said. Hold on to what is good. Stay away from every kind of evil"* (1 Thessalonians 5:20–22). The admonition to test everything that is said in prophetic contexts implies that many false things are spoken in religious circles.

The apostle John added,

Dear friends, do not believe everyone who claims to speak by the Spirit. You must test them to see if the spirit they have comes from God. For there are many false prophets in the world. This is how we know if they have the Spirit of God: If a person claiming to be a prophet acknowledges that Jesus Christ came in a real body, that person has the Spirit of God. But if someone claims to be a prophet and does not acknowledge the truth about Jesus, that person is not from God. Such a person has the spirit of the Antichrist, which you

*heard is coming into the world and indeed is
already here.*

*But you belong to God, my dear children.
You have already won a victory over those
people, because the Spirit who lives in you is
greater than the spirit who lives in the world.*
(1 John 4:1–4)

For John, the critical issue regarding spiritual proclamations was speaking truthfully about Christ. In his historical context, that meant a proper understanding of the Incarnation, embracing both the full deity and full humanity of Christ. First and second century Christians growing up in Greek culture had a hard time with that one.

But the main focus of the passage is still applicable today—false prophets (of which there are many) deliver messages that are incongruent with the truth about Jesus. A significant component of discernment always involves aligning the message with everything we know to be true about Jesus from the Word of God. As the apostle John said in the book of Revelation, *"For the essence of prophecy is to give a clear witness for Jesus"* (Revelation 19:10). False prophets and teachers will usually mess up in this area.

The Bible firmly acknowledges the presence of false prophets and teachers nestled amongst the true people of God (2 Peter 2). Old Testament Law subjected false prophets to capital punishment. New Testament writers warned believers of the severe punishment awaiting false teachers in the future judgment (Jude 4–15).

The presence of false teachers within the church implies that there are wrong ways to pursue God, ways that start off looking sincere but end in destruction. The job description of true followers of Jesus Christ does not just include tenets of firm dedication and pious devotion—it involves discernment. Those who want to pursue God properly must discriminate between truth and falsehood. They must be willing to separate the evil from the good. Otherwise, they are vulnerable to being spiritually misguided. A cursory glance around today's spiritual landscape bears witness to the fact that such a fate is quite common.

Normally, when we think of being misguided, we envision the deceptive villain as residing outside Christian circles with no apparent interest in God. But so much deception, and the need for discernment, happens within the arms of the church structure. The deception is close by. The deceivers may even be friends.

Many Christians are daunted by the thought of discerning *messages from the Lord.* They feel inadequate or unqualified to determine what type of spirit is behind someone's *sacred proclamations.* They don't want to *"quench the Spirit"* (1 Thessalonians 5:19, NASB). They are afraid to blaspheme the Holy Spirit, which Christ referred to as an unpardonable sin (Luke 12:10). And they fear coming off as overly judgmental (usually based on quoting Matthew 7:1 without reading the next four verses).

Humanly speaking, these fears seem well-grounded. But they do not preclude the need for true followers of Christ to discriminate, to test what people are saying about God and about the journey that leads to a closer relationship with him.

It's tricky. We must deal with people who say things like *God told me…*But we need not be intimidated by this phrase. Just because someone uses it does not mean God has truly spoken to that person. Jeremiah 23 records the Lord's own frustration with people who were saying their words were from him when they were actually originating from their own imaginations. Jeremiah warned these careless-tongued individuals by saying, *"But stop using this phrase, 'prophecy from the Lord.' For people are using it to give authority to their own ideas, turning upside down the words of our God, the living God, the Lord of Heaven's Armies"* (Jeremiah 23:36).

It is quite common for people to amplify the caliber of their spiritual thoughts by claiming their message comes directly from God. In Jeremiah's day, God called these people *"smooth-tongued"* (23:31) *"prophets of deceit, inventing everything they say"* (23:26). His verdict was clear: *"They proceed to tell lies in my name"* (23:25). Jeremiah 23 also records the Lord facetiously encouraging these false prophets to go ahead and keep telling their false tales, because in comparison to the true words of

God, their lies will be exposed for what they are—mere chaff compared to the grain of the true words of God (23:28). For, *"'Does not my word burn like fire?' says the Lord. 'Is it not like a mighty hammer that smashes a rock to pieces?'"* (23:29). The true Word of God is powerful, strong in both intensity and efficacy. False messages are more fluffy.

So, discernment is complicated. You might have to challenge someone who claims God is speaking through them. But it's also delicate. Within the message of a false teacher lie kernels of truth. Believers must learn to sift through the content of the message in order to identify that which is false and then be prepared to expose the error.

Having said all that, spiritual judgment is not rocket science. All believers are capable of doing it to some degree. But bear in mind, there is a supernatural aspect of spiritual testing that cannot be fully explained or written in the pages of a book. And there is the aspect of spiritual discernment as being a spiritual gift. But it is not super-mystical. Some of its requirements are obvious. It entails humility and a dependence on the Holy Spirit. It likewise necessitates meditation and prayer. But most of all, it has a lot to do with our own personal acquaintance with, and adherence to, the Scriptures.

When we hear someone say *Thus saith the Lord,* there are a number of questions we need to ask ourselves. Does the Holy Spirit within me affirm the truth of this message? Does it jibe with what God has already revealed within the infrastructure of Kingdom teaching? Does it compel me to become more like Christ? Is it more in line with my personal preferences and good feelings than with dying to self? Does it serve me or God primarily? Is it super weird?

If it is a message that primarily promotes my health and wealth and is not focused on Christ, there's a good chance it's not from God. If it involves the spectacular or the miraculous to the neglect of sacrifice or the cross, it may not be genuinely divine (remember, the devil also does miracles). If it is accompanied by the purchase of a specially blessed religious artifact, you might want to proceed with caution. If it does not comply with the gospel message of Christ or with the preeminence of the power of the Savior's blood, then it is peripheral at best and false at worst.

Jesus said one of the main roles of the Holy Spirit is that of conviction—to *"convict the world of its sin, and of God's righteousness, and of the coming judgment"* (John 16:8). Part of spiritual discernment involves determining whether a supposed message from the Lord carries more confirmation than conviction. Is the message more about something God has for you or more about the conviction of sin in your life?

John F. Kennedy's 1961 presidential inaugural address was so powerful because self-sacrifice always rings truer than selfishness—*"Ask not what your country can do for you. Ask what you can do for your country."* True messages from God and the true pursuit of God always relate more to what you can do for God's Kingdom, rather than what God can do for your temporal benefit.

But even though discernment is necessary, not all believers are equally adept at it. Young believers or those new in the faith may not have the biblical training that is essential to discriminate spiritual claims. In Acts 19, the apostle Paul met some new Christian believers who had not even heard of the Holy Spirit. Consequently, they needed some instruction in the truth about the full message of the gospel of Jesus Christ and the work of the Holy Spirit since the Lord's ascension into heaven.

However, mere knowledge of the Scriptures is not enough. A lifestyle of consistent obedience to the Word of God is *the* component that separates the spiritually mature from the babies. True spiritual wisdom in a believer is directly proportional to the level of obedience practiced by that individual. The Psalmist said, *"I am even wiser than my elders, for I have kept your commandments"* (Psalm 119:100). Many know what God has said. Only the wise few obey consistently. The writer of Hebrews concurs when he refers to mature believers as those *"who because of practice have their senses trained to discern good and evil"* (Hebrews 5:14, NASB).

Years of faithful obedience to God's Word give one the ability to spot those beliefs and practices that are merely human or demonic in origin. As in the field of currency security, spotting a counterfeit is best done by fully knowing the nature of the true original. When you know the truth so well, you can spot the fakes. And when you can spot the fakes, you will less likely be deceived or sidetracked in your pursuit of God.

Sinatra

I'M NOT A BIG SINATRA FAN, BUT WHENEVER HIS NAME is mentioned, my mind goes to the lyrics of one of this crooner's more famous hits. In this captivating tune, Sinatra reflects on his earthly achievements from the standpoint of his life coming to a close. Celebrating the fact of living a full life and approaching countless experiences with great confidence and gusto, the singer concludes with the powerful line *"I faced it all and I stood tall and did it my way."*[6]

The remarkable melody of this tune may be semi-divine in its power and emotion, but the lyrics are horribly human. They reek of foolish confidence and irrational self-reliance.

---

6 "Frank Sinatra My Way Lyrics," LyricsFreak, accessed September 8, 2012, http://www.lyricsfreak.com/f/frank+sinatra/my+way_20056378.html

The most common trail for the average person is to live independently from God. Those who ignore or reject the claims of Christ on their lives proceed autonomously through the highways and byways of life, believing that a self-directed and self-sufficient existence is the pinnacle of human accomplishment.

Unfortunately, such independence and self-reliance also creeps into sacred circles of God-seekers. One of the most common temptations in the pursuit of God is to do it *my way.* Something in our flesh resists submission to God. We don't like to surrender to him, especially when the terms of peace are disagreeable to our selfish human nature.

Instead of accepting what God says, we adapt his message to our personal needs. We interpret divine principles of attaining godliness in ways that make sense to us. And when they don't make sense to our rational minds, we ignore them or invent other principles that are more logical. Instead of eating what's on the menu, we barge back into the kitchen and create new dishes that we deem more palatable.

As is hopefully evident by now, the purpose of this book is to create a paradigm for understanding the proper pursuit of God. This paradigm helps us see how people in the past and present have done it improperly, mixing sinful slants into the journey of knowing God more intimately, a practice I have been calling *sacred sedition.* And this paradigm is not intended merely as a topic for theological discussion. It should compel us to examine our own lives more carefully, thinking about the paths we have chosen to attain a deeper relationship with God. Are we doing it his way, or our way? Better yet, let's answer the question more personally—am *I* doing it his way, or my way?

Let me offer three ways that sincere seekers Sinatra-cize the gospel, doing it *their way.*

Some people view their relationship with God from a perspective of relative human behavior. Their pursuit of God consists of using a humanly devised spiritual thermometer that measures their performance in comparison to the average person in the world. Their line of thinking goes something like this:

I became a Christian at a Bible camp when I was nine. Since then, I've lived a pretty good life, better than most. I am thoughtful and considerate. I am one of the nicer people at work. I don't steal, abuse alcohol or cheat on my spouse. I am raising my family in the church and I give money in the offering plate every week. I even sponsor children in Third World countries. In comparison to the majority of people in the world, I'm doing good enough. No, in fact, I'm doing very well. Fellowship with God demands holiness, and I would say I'm on the right track. I don't see many people around me doing more than I'm doing to please God.

This version of *my way* to God provides a contentment found in comparing oneself to the utter sinfulness of the world in general. These seekers find solace in the fact that they are doing it right because they are better than most. The full concept of God's absolute holiness is never considered. Righteousness is measured by human standards mixed with a few biblical precepts.

For these Sinatra-teers (sorry Mickey), spiritual maturity is something they determine. Once they have reached a level of personal behavior that feels adequate, they retire in comfort on their self-constructed spiritual plateaus. Pursuing God is defined more by man-made outward behaviors than by a meaningful relationship with him where there is ongoing communication that leads to deeper conviction and perpetual repentance. Instead of recognizing that being *"mature in the Lord"* means *"measuring up to the full and complete standard of Christ"* (Ephesians 4:13), they foolishly *"measure themselves by themselves"* (2 Corinthians 10:12, NASB).

Strike one!

Other sincere seekers Sinatra-cize the gospel by selecting and adhering to only specific aspects of the Christian message. These people put great stock in their ability to make personal choices about the exact unfolding of their spiritual journey. They will design their own route to God using bits and pieces of his Word. Instead of surrendering fully to God and submitting to everything he has revealed, these

Sinatra   91

seekers will decide what is important to them and what is not.

Their line of thinking goes something like this:

I know that I'm a Christian; there's no reason to make a big public scene about it. I go to church when I feel like it. Just to drag myself there when I'm tired or not in the mood would be hypocritical. Jesus doesn't like hypocrites.

I know the Bible well enough. I don't need to read it all the time. Besides, the Bible was written a long time ago to people very different than me so it's not entirely meaningful to everyone in every situation. I can figure out what parts apply to me. There's no need to take things too seriously; that's how those nutty cults get started. Christianity is mostly about being a good person. There's no need to get carried away and scare people off with crazy fanaticism.

Christian service? I do what I can. I live a good life; people can see that. God knows I'm really busy at work. There's just no way I have the time to commit to church activities. I don't want to sign up and then have to quit; that would be irresponsible. Besides, that church stuff is more for women. Things will be all right in the end; God knows my heart.

What these folks are embracing on their path to God is a thinned-out version of Christianity. To avoid the dangers of fanatical carbs, they prefer to sip *Jesus Lite*. This paradigm for spiritual progress is rooted strongly in human confidence. They are quite assured in their ability to pinpoint what matters to them. They will dabble in the Scriptures when they feel like it, pruning out that which doesn't interest them. They know best.

These people may occasionally be intrigued by a solidly biblical convicting sermon, but they continue to treat the Word of God as a buffet. They pick and choose what they want. And their interest in messages from God is more intellectual than personal. They hear God speak, but like the Parable of the Four Soils, the seed falls on rocky soil and produces no lasting fruit.

People operating with a watered-down form of Christianity think they are making decisions based on their own choosing. They believe their choices are satisfactory because they have good intentions. In reality, they are being molded by the influence of others and the pressures of this world.

People in this camp, fashioning their own way to God through their own personal judgment, lack a strong desire to know the real Jesus or the fullness of God. Without even realizing it, they may have even abandoned the simple faith and total trust of their youth, exchanging it for a Christian life that holds *"to a form of godliness, although they have denied its power"* (2 Timothy 3:5, NASB).

Strike two!

Another way people pursue God in their own manner involves an all-consuming devotion to human rationalism. Sincere seekers of this persuasion place reason above faith. Faith will only be implemented once human reason has been satisfied. These are people who, for various reasons, cannot accept certain aspects of God's Word by faith because they seem too illogical. In this process, they elevate their thinking to the level of God's thinking. They treat God as a peer whose input into spiritual matters is valuable but only equal to theirs. They worship the supremacy of human logic over simple trust in God.

Their line of thinking goes something like this:

I want to believe and fully commit to Christ, but there are just so many things that I don't get about the Bible. There is so much killing in the Old Testament. Then there's all those contradictions people talk about. God knows I really want to believe in him, but the Bible is so confusing. Until I can get my head around all these puzzling things, I'm not prepared to jump in with both feet. That's not asking too much, is it?

Surely the God of the universe is a rational God. Nature is bathed in reason. Mathematics is the language of his creative work, and there's nothing more logical or predictable than math. He created me in his image and made me a rational being. He understands that I need answers that fit into the mind he gave me. Certainly, he doesn't want me to throw out my brain to follow him. I need some better explanations before I will feel comfortable to proceed any further.

I feel for people of this persuasion because I could be tempted to dance with them. I'm a fairly logical guy (much to the irritation of my wife when we argue). I know how human reason can seem so right. I know how faith in God, at times, can seem like a leap off a cliff.

But I also know that I am a marvelous and spectacular creation. It's easy for me to believe that someone bigger than me is keeping my heart beating. And I also recognize that for human reason to even exist, a more powerful being than me must be running the system that makes its existence possible. For these reasons, I am convinced that human thinking, like all things in creation, must bow before God. My brain must surrender to its maker.

Genuine seekers who stick with the supremacy of human reason over faith are more concerned with getting all their ducks in a row than with submitting to God. Until they can sense the logic of Christian theology, they are not prepared to accept it fully. That is a humanly devised pathway to God, so it is guaranteed to fail.

God's ways are not our ways. His thinking is so much higher than our natural thinking. As Francis Chan presents in *Erasing Hell,* we would never come up with some of the ideas that God has conceived. He is so far above us. We insult him and embarrass ourselves by placing our thinking above his.

Unfortunately, this path of deifying benevolent human logic is not just for skeptics. It's also navigated by well-meaning Christians. Some contemporary theologians, presenting themselves as fully in the game of faith, proceed to eliminate certain doctrines of traditional Christian belief because—wait for it—they seem unreasonable.

Take the doctrine of hell, for instance. Rational human thought has trouble with what the Bible says about hell. The concept is hard to stomach when viewed from our natural mindset. The logistics of hell seem unreasonable. How can a loving God subject any human to such a fate?

But when we proceed to make proclamations like *God's not like that* or *I can't believe in a God who would do that,* we have errantly subjected our pursuit of God to liberal human reasoning. We are no longer seeking the one true God. We have made *ourselves* to be God and demoted him to be our servant. We might as well call him Jeeves instead of Yahweh. Down there he can do the bidding of our rational minds.

Strike three!

Batter's out!

People love to say *I can find my own way to God.*

Really? Are we that arrogant? Can our individual talent and character get the job done? We, who are dependent on God for every single breath we take, can forge our own path to him? How do we have the wherewithal to do that? How did we gain this ability? According to God's Word and every newscast for the past millennia, the human heart is wicked. There is no one who naturally seeks after God. All have turned aside (Romans 3).

To say that I can find my own path to God is just as ridiculous as a toddler saying, *I can find my own way up Mount Everest. I don't need any Sherpa guides or advice from Sir Edmund Hillary. I can handle it myself. In the end, it'll be great to say, I did it my way.*

Sorry Frank. You may have sold a lot of records, but you, like so many misguided God-seekers of every generation, are celebrating creation over the Creator. And so you, and they, are wrong.

I don't get closer to God by doing it my way. I can only enter into an intimate relationship with my Heavenly Father by doing it his way—the way of suffering and sacrifice, the way of cross-bearing, the way of dying to self, the way that involves putting Christ ahead of absolutely everything in my life.

Smooth

ONE OF THE MORE RECENT TRENDS IN CHRISTIAN writing is a line of books that possess what I would call a heavy *cool factor.* Some of their authors are younger men who made decisions to follow Jesus in their youth. However, over time they became jaded by the supposedly rigid presentations of Christianity in their parents' churches, and they have now been reborn into a new understanding, one that they feel represents Christianity as it was intended to be.

These new authors appear to be offering a fresh perspective on the gospel, one that fits with the freer consumption of alcohol and the smoking of the occasional cigar or pipe for the purpose of punctuating the fact that we are free in Christ. Their colorful and breezy writings typically resist the supposed legalism of traditional Christianity and encourage readers to embrace a fresher glimpse of the *real Jesus,* a guy who would feel very comfortable in a pub. They are quick to remind us that Jesus turned water into really good wine and loved to party with sinners, all in the hope that we truly grasp the liberating nature of God's grace.

This version of pursuing God seems to be guided by intelligent literary creations characterized by compassionate reasoning and clever word imagery. The writing is artsy, tasty and cool. The literature is very smooth.

In my opinion, some of these writings end up causing more harm than good on the path of pursuing God. The books become popular, even in mainstream culture, but may fail to truly lead people to God in a meaningful and enduring fashion. Even though the books are fun to read and pleasingly inspirational, the movement appears to be more about good, interesting writing than about a deeper knowledge of God. These authors give the impression of offering a new perspective on old truth but sometimes disregard the rigors of the cost of discipleship as Jesus defined it.

Christ's message was not rocket science—*If you're ready to pay the price of absolute surrender and obedience, come and follow me to God.* It may be hard to do, but it's not hard to comprehend. We don't need crafty metaphors to get it. We don't need witty humor to take the edge off. We don't need drawn-out discussions on the merits of Christians drinking beer. And we certainly don't need images in our minds that God may actually be an African-American woman of substantial girth.

Contemporary Christianity is certainly well-entertained by the easy-listening sounds of emerging and emergent church writers. Both groups have offered writings that are unique to the Christian literature genre. Personally, I am more disturbed by the latter than the former. *Emerging* church thinkers endorse an innovative approach to presenting the gospel for the twenty-first century. They are critical of the traditional church because they feel it has been too legalistic and has failed to keep in step with contemporary society and culture. They want to present a Christianity that is more accessible and relevant to people who would otherwise have no interest in the church or in Christ himself. Emerging church writers believe we must do church differently if we want to remain viable. It's hard not to agree with the general premise of emerging church thought—the church needs to be aware of cultural changes and make a solid effort to present Christ in ways that are actually heard by the younger generations. Otherwise, when the old folks die off, there will be very few people of Christian faith left in our western civilization. It is true—the gospel message can still be presented in a pure and undefiled manner on Facebook and Twitter or in blogs.

I do believe emerging church writers have good intentions about bringing people into the Kingdom through inventive strategies and stimulating liturgical imagery. However, when the smoke clears from the room, sometimes the gospel message presented on their pages is not true to all the words of Christ. They present interesting quotable quotes on getting to know the *real Jesus* but sometimes come up a bit short on cross-bearing, dying to self and suffering for Christ.

When considering the merit of emerging church writings, it is important to remember that such literature is predominantly a phenomenon of Western civilization. Only in North America do we have so much wealth, comfort and time on our hands that we are able to muse about new ways to express our Christian faith. We have become jaded with the simple precepts of following Christ and being totally obedient to him. Our Christian brothers and sisters in Iran or West Java know nothing of this sort of theological angst. For them, the simple words of Jesus ring true on a daily basis—*"Everyone will hate you because you are my followers"* (Luke 21:17).

Emergent church writers, on the other hand, present a far greater challenge to Christ's gospel than their emerging counterparts. Instead of just pushing for a Christianity that is more applicable and culturally connecting, the *emergent village* (or *emergent stream* as it is sometimes called) colors way outside the traditional evangelical lines. These revisionists are theologically liberal, openly questioning whether evangelical doctrine is appropriate for the postmodern world. Emergent writers call many Christian tenets into question. *Was Jesus really God? Is there truly such a place as hell and would God send his creatures there? Is sex outside marriage wrong? Is homosexuality really a sin?*

Under the banner of pursuing God, emergent writers appear to be tracking a different deity than the one Christ and the New Testament writers spoke of. In their desire to be more authentic and less offensive, these thinkers are being led away from Christ. Jesus clearly stated that there are not multiple paths to God—*"No one can come to the Father except through me"* (John 14:6). Opposing the exclusivity of Christ's words, the main idea of the emergent village seems to be that Jesus is a super nice guy who simply wants to embrace all people of different faiths. And because they write with such exceptional style and literary brilliance, their message sounds believable.

There is no denying it—these emergent writers are humanly smart, really smart. They are phenomenal communicators who write with elegance and imagination (e.g., Brian McLaren's *Why Did Moses, Jesus, the Buddha, and Mohammed Cross the Road?*, 2012). And they are genuinely nice guys themselves. They look and sound very loving. They care for the plight of the poor and the oppressed in this world. They seek social justice and world ecology. These are not bad men at all.

Of course, their message of universalism is attractive. *Ecumenical* and *embracing* are feel-good words. Humanly speaking, I would like to make them my life song as well. What's better than a guy who just wants to bring everybody together so we can all get along and solve the problems of the world? What's more courageous than a kind man or woman attempting to build bridges between people with ideological differences? But it's not that simple when you're dealing with divine revelation to a sinful humanity. Nice humans don't make the rules. God does.

In these smooth emergent writings championing benevolence and solidarity, traditional Christianity is viewed as predominantly drunk with derision for sinners and hostility for people of other faiths. The reader is asked to accept a compassionate paradigm of universalism and to abandon the intolerance of a vague group of fanatics referred to as *most Christians you know*. These sophisticated liberals promote the wholehearted love of Christ but ignore his more challenging sayings that sound exclusive and thin—*"You can enter God's Kingdom only through the narrow gate. The highway to hell is broad, and its gate is wide for the many who choose that way"* (Matthew 7:13).

I, and most Christians that I know, have no desire to strong-arm anyone or to create barriers in the name of God. We don't hate people of other faiths. We love them. We don't preach Christ to them because we think we are right and superior while they are wrong and inferior. We want everyone to come to God through faith in Christ because Jesus said that's the only way. The emergent paradigm fails to recognize the reality of spiritual deception. *All sincere religious people seeking God must be doing it right, because they're seeking God. Right?*

Wrong!

Sincerity is not the determining factor, and kindness is not the authority on these matters. Christ is. And from my reading of the Gospels, Jesus is the most exclusive Christian thinker I know. He has to be; he's God. In true Yahweh fashion, he claimed to be a whole lot of I AMs—the living water, the bread of life, the light of the world, the door, the good shepherd, the Son of God, the resurrection and the life, the true vine, the King of the Jews, the way, the truth and the life. In the Old Testament, God made himself more personal to humanity by telling us his name—Yahweh, I AM. In the New Testament, Jesus used numerous metaphors to show us who he was—the Great I AM. He is everything to man and the only way to God. If a mere human said these things, it would be conceitedly egocentric and false. When Jesus said them, it was truth.

In speaking to earnest and devoted people of other religions (e.g., Judaism), Jesus did not hesitate to say that their true Father was not Abraham but the devil (John 8:44). And he proceeded to explain to them that they were in their deceived state because they were connected with *"the father of lies"* (John 8:44). Instead of trying to build bridges to find commonalities between himself and these other religious thinkers, Jesus simply said they were wrong. He told them that even on their best days, they were just whitewashed tombs full of dead men's bones (Matthew 23:27). He often made people mad. Sometimes when Jesus was done his sermon, the congregation would pick up rocks to stone him (John 8:59, 10:31).

In their pursuit of God, emergent writers appear to be challenging the deity of Christ. In place of the true Messiah, they glorify human benevolence. Their god is not Yahweh. Their deity is a human intellect that wants to be nice and not offend anyone. When I read their writings or watch their videos on YouTube, essentially what I hear emergent thinkers saying is the following: *God is love, and my interpretation of what that means is supreme.*

Yikes!

Let's face it. Jesus made it very clear that his gospel *is* offensive. He called both the morally corrupt and the seemingly morally elite to a place of humility and dependence on God. He equated lust with adultery and hate with murder. He said that no one is good, except for God, and that those with the best intentions of following God have actually murdered his very messengers. The apostle Paul agreed. He spoke unmistakably of the offensive nature of the message of the cross (Galatians 5:11). Even back in the days of Elijah, the feisty prophet who didn't pull punches about the exclusivity of Yahweh was referred to as a *"troublemaker"* (1 Kings 18:17).

These smooth and talented emergent writers don't want any trouble. They just want to be really nice guys. They try to make the gospel more appetizing by deviating from the tougher words of Jesus. This makes their contribution to pursuing God all that much more seditious. They appear sacred, but actually they remain in a state of rebellion against God without even knowing it.

In writing to the church at Rome almost 2,000 years ago, the apostle Paul seems to be talking specifically about emergent liberals when he says,

Watch out for people who cause divisions and upset people's faith by teaching things contrary to what you have been taught. Stay away from them. Such people are not serving Christ our Lord; they are serving their own personal interests. By smooth talk and glowing words they deceive innocent people. (Romans 16:17–18)

Emerging Christianity is exactly right in its desire to maintain an orthodox gospel presented in more accessible and relevant ways. Throughout history, the Kingdom of God has always been furthered by adapting to contemporary technological and cultural advancements (e.g., the printing press in the fifteenth century). At the risk of sounding trite, emerging church writers just need to make sure they don't throw out the baby with the bath water.

Emergent liberals, on the other hand, just need to repent and return to the whole counsel of God instead of clinging solely to parts they like. They might also do well to heed the apostle Paul's warning to the church in Colossae: *"Don't let anyone capture you with empty philosophies and high-sounding nonsense that come from human thinking and from the spiritual powers of this world, rather than from Christ"* (Colossians 2:8).

Wrong

BESIDES THE EMERGENT VILLAGE, THERE ARE A NUMBER of other spurious movements within contemporary Christianity that bear the markings of false teaching. Their presence should not surprise us, though, because God told us they would appear—*"Now the Holy Spirit tells us clearly that in the last times some will turn away from the true faith; they will follow deceptive spirits and teachings that come from demons"* (1 Timothy 4:1).

To better understand the origin of this most recent fragmentation of Christianity into its present confusing state, a little church history is in order. The sixteenth-century Protestant Reformation called for a different Christianity than what Roman Catholicism had offered for centuries. In this new paradigm, authority was based solely on Scripture, and salvation was by faith alone. Birthed in the intellectual milieu of Europe's late Renaissance, it's no surprise that the Protestant Reformation was focused on developing new and logical comprehensive systems of theology.

Even though the concept of the individual priesthood of the believer splintered Christendom into several denominations, these reformers wanted to get their doctrines right—all of them. Great emphasis was placed on the supremacy of the mind over the heart. Protestant Reformers were consumed with determining the truth and then declaring that truth through the preaching of the Word of God. The role of the heart in the Reformed tradition was simply to respond to God and his truth as it was preached from the pulpit and enacted in the sacraments.

In the eighteenth century, a further splintering of Protestant Christianity occurred with the birth of evangelicalism. Influenced by the Methodist revivals in England and the Pietism movement in Germany, evangelicalism had four foci—the importance of a life-changing personal conversion experience, high regard for the Bible, a stress on the sacrifice of Christ on the cross, and the spreading of the gospel through world missions.[7] And in response to the need for unity in order to spread the gospel, evangelicals highlighted doctrines they could all agree upon. Once the theological shuffling was done, ecclesiology

---

7 David W. Babbington, Evangelicalism in Modern Britain: A History from 1730s to the 1980s [Grand Rapids: Baker, 1989], 2–3

(i.e., the nature of the church) and the sacraments got left in the dust. Church structure and practice soon became a free-for-all. New denominations and mission organizations popped up by the hundreds, even thousands.

Under the influence of nineteenth century Romanticism, evangelicalism also developed a new perspective on the nature and role of the human heart in religious matters. Where the heart was traditionally perceived as deceptive and untrustworthy, it now became the judge of spiritual truth. And instead of the heart responding to truth as the Reformers believed, the heart now became the barometer of truth. When the heart is warmed, this is an indication that it is experiencing something true. Like the Romantic poets, musicians and artists of the day, it was believed that in order to bypass the cold dead reasoning and confusion of rationalism (i.e., eighteenth century theology and science), emotions were needed to truly touch reality. In evangelicalism, reason became the servant of the heart. The arousal of such passion and purposeful mission orientation led to further disunity within the Christian church. More and more denominational distinctives were forged as people followed their hearts in their individual pursuit of God.

The greatest splintering of evangelicalism into its most bizarre bits has certainly occurred in the last forty years. With its Romantic preoccupation of encountering truth through emotional experience, the heart now judges what is true about God. In other words, my heart is my own personal truth detector. And with our weak and wicked hearts as our truth detectors, Christians have become more vulnerable to the teachings of false prophets.

With this philosophical drift, many sincere people now pursue God wrongly without realizing it—lots of heart and very little head. Like flies to honey, they are attracted to the positive and exciting emotions of faith-healing and miracle-worker crusades. They are terribly hungry for God to move in their lives so they bite at attractive lures. Their hearts are warmed by attending particular meetings or churches that seem to exhibit God's presence (i.e., loud manifestations, participants falling under the power of God and ending up on the floor, *holy* laughter and/or falling jewels, gold dust or feathers). In an almost drug-addicted state, countless seekers devote their time and pour their money into the schemes of televangelists who promise health and wealth and spectacular spiritual experiences (e.g., trips to heaven), all in the name of *just wanting everything God has for me.*

But here's the problem. Because many of these more recent divergent offshoots of evangelicalism have strayed too far from the Word of God, they cannot be deemed anything but heretical.

Of course, not every off-shoot is automatically counterfeit. Evangelical branches like First Wave Pentecostalism (early twentieth century) were preoccupied with an outpouring of the Holy Spirit like that in the book of Acts. Though there may be some debate regarding their doctrinal distinctives (e.g., baptism of the Holy Spirit with evidence of speaking in tongues), the first Pentecostals still held to the same gospel message as traditional evangelicalism (i.e., a sinful humanity needing to repent in order to appropriate the saving blood of Jesus). And even within the peculiarities of the early Pentecostal movement, its leaders were cognizant of the danger of spiritual deception. Amidst what he considered to be a genuine move of God, *"Pentecostal leader Charles Parham also described manifestations of barking like a dog, braying like a donkey, crowing like a rooster, and contortions and fits as demonic."*[8]

But today's charismatic radicals seem to lack this discernment. In their zeal without knowledge (Romans 10:2), these latest offshoots of evangelicalism have diminished the supremacy of the cross of Christ and replaced it with three new foundational pillars—Word of Faith teaching, Apostolic/Prophetic Revival and Prosperity Theology. All three are closely related and, at times, overlap each other. Most of the time, all three incorporate teachings that are strange and experiences that are nothing short of weird.

---

8 "Slain in What Spirit," InPlainSite.org, accessed December 9, 2012, http://www.inplainsite.org/html/slain_in_the_spirit_1.html

The Word of Faith movement has its origins in the writings of Phineas P. Quimby (1802–1866), the father of New Thought. New Thought believes *God* is an impersonal intelligent force within all of us. Its fundamental teaching is that spirit is more real and more powerful than matter and that the mind has the power to heal the body if it thinks right thoughts.

Influenced by a college education steeped in New Thought, Essek W. Kenyon (1867–1948) developed the key aspects of Word of Faith. Besides some outlandish tenets—humans taking on the nature of Satan at the Fall and Jesus dying spiritually on the cross, needing himself to be reborn—Kenyon taught that God created the universe and everything in it by speaking faith-filled words.[9] As little gods ourselves, we supposedly are to do the same. Consequently, health and wealth are obtainable by the believer's positive confession.

Riding (or perhaps driving) the wave of charismatic revival after World War II (often referred to as the Latter Rain Revival or Second Wave Pentecostalism), William Branham (1909–1965) championed Word of Faith doctrine and demonstrated its *truth* through a vast healing and prophetic ministry

---

9 Neil Rivalland, "Did Jesus Die Spiritually, His Spirit Become Re-Created, And He Become Born Again?" Apologetics Coordination Team, accessed February 18, 2013, http://www.deceptioninthechurch.com/word-faith2.html

(a movement known as Healing Revivalism). Apart from his bizarre beliefs—Eve had sex with the serpent in the Garden, the doctrine of the Trinity is of the devil, he himself is the angel of Revelation 3:14[10]—Branham made many prophetic predictions that failed to come true (e.g., all denominations would be consumed by the World Council of Churches in 1977).

The father of modern Word of Faith is unanimously recognized as Kenneth Hagin (1917–2003). Although he claimed to have received his teachings directly from God, they appear to be taken right out of the doctrines of Essek W. Kenyon. Currently, the two greatest campaigners for the movement are Kenneth Copeland and Benny Hinn.

Besides the doctrines already mentioned (positive confession, mankind is actually divine, Jesus died a spiritual death on the cross and was tortured by Satan in hell), Word of Faith preachers teach that Jesus completely emptied himself of his deity when he came to earth. He then lived his life solely as a human, performing all his miracles through the power of God. Consequently, those who are saved should be able to do exactly what Jesus did because he supposedly possessed no advantage over us in

10 "William Branham Teachings," Christian Debatorial Works, accessed on February 18, 2013, http://members.tripod.com/debatorial_works/id300.htm

our current state. All we need to do is speak words of faith and we, like God, can create anything we want (especially health and wealth).

Word of Faith also teaches that prayer is the act of man giving God permission to do something on earth. Myles Munroe, president of Bahamas Faith Ministries International, states, *"Nothing has God ever done on earth without a human giving him access."*[11]

In their perverted minds they believe, and convince others, that God can only do what we give him license to do. And if we ask in faith, he is required to answer. It makes me wonder if they have ever read the Psalms—*"But our God is in the heavens; He does whatever He pleases"* (Psalm 115:3).

Further misrepresentations of the nature of God are found in the words of Kenneth Copeland, who says,

> *"I was shocked when I found out who the biggest failure in the Bible actually is…The biggest one is God…I mean, He lost His top-ranking, most anointed angel; the first man He ever created; the first woman He ever created; the whole earth and all the Fullness therein; a*

---

11 "Exposing The False Teaching of the Word of Faith and Prosperity Gospel Preachers, Clip #1," Worldview Weekend Tube, accessed December 9, 2012, http://www.worldviewweekend.com/worldview-tube/play.php?id=cwnVideo-4460

third of the angels, at least—that's a big loss, man...Now, the reason you don't think of God as a failure is He never said He's a failure. And you're not a failure till you say you're one."[12]

Instead of dignifying this sacrilege with a response, we will just move on.

The second pillar of this unorthodox fragmentation of evangelicalism is the New Apostolic Reformation and the Prophetic Movement (referred to as Third Wave Pentecostalism). The basic thesis of this joint movement is that God is presently restoring the lost offices of church governance, namely that of apostles and prophets, accompanied by great signs and wonders. Some of those who shaped the current Apostolic-Prophetic Movement in America were led by Mike Bickle and were based in Kansas City, Missouri. These men, including Bob Jones, Paul Cain, Rick Joyner and John Paul Jackson, became known as the *Kansas City Prophets*. From there, the movement spread to the Vineyard Church near the Toronto International Airport (called the Toronto Blessing) and then to Lakeland, Florida, under the *ministry* of a flamboyant man named Todd Bentley.

12 "Praise-a-Thon" program on TBN [April 1988], "Trinity Broadcasting Network," Hard Truth, www.theforbiddenknowledge.com/hardtruth/tbn_network.htm

Besides the usual charismatic manifestations associated with their meetings (i.e., speaking in tongues and being slain in the spirit), these self-proclaimed prophets claim to be able to heal indiscriminately and brag about having had incredible spiritual experiences (e.g., accessing heavenly portals at will and interacting with personal angels).

These neo-charismatic spiritual leaders also assert that they receive divine instruction and teaching directly from God. Some of these *divine* teachings are fairly peculiar. Benny Hinn claimed that God told him Adam flew to the moon and that women were originally designed to give birth out of their sides.[13] Some of their *divine* instructions are completely whacked out. Todd Bentley said God told him to kick an old woman in the face with his biker boots as a means of healing her.[14]

Claiming to speak with divine authority, these counterfeits are clearly false prophets (Deuteronomy 18:21–22). Their predictions continually fail to materialize (e.g., Kenneth Copeland's prophecy that

---

13 Hank Hanegraaff, "What's Wrong with the Word Faith Movement? (Part One)," The Christian Research Institute, accessed February 18, 2013, http://www.equip.org/articles/whats-wrong-with-the-word-faith-movement-part-one/

14 Ben Ellery, "MP calls for ban on tattooed preacher who 'cures' cancer by kicking people in the face," Mail Online, August 5, 2012, http://www.dailymail.co.uk/news/article-2183860/Todd-Bentley-MP-calls-ban-tattooed-preacher-cures-cancer-kicking-people-face.html

Islam would fall in 1995), and their lives habitually display questionable moral character (e.g., Todd Bentley's affair with his ministry partner and Bob Jones' sexual misconduct with women in 1991).

When investigative journalism seeks to confirm the claims of these elite prophets regarding crusade healings or incidences of raising people from the dead, no single case can ever be authentically verified.[15] Instead of worshiping God in spirit and truth, the Apostolic-Prophetic Movement promotes a circus-like environment characterized by materialism (i.e., falling gold dust and jewels), wild manifestations, chaotic screaming, convulsions, and animal noises as well as a good dose of *holy* laughter (particularly courtesy of Rodney Howard-Browne—a.k.a. the *Holy Ghost Bartender*).[16]

Instead of heeding the Scriptural command to *"be sober in all things"* (2 Timothy 4:5, NASB), this new brand of charismatic exuberance prefers spiritual intoxication that fills its participants with feelings of love and euphoria while they abandon the mind. Some of these new mystics like John Crowder even go so far as to speak of participating in the

15 "Benny Hinn," Wikipedia, accessed February 18, 2013, http://en.wikipedia.org/wiki/Benny_Hinn

16 "Rodney Howard-Browne," Wikipedia, accessed December 16, 2012, http://en.wikipedia.org/wiki/Rodney_Howard-Browne

heavy drunken glory of God.[17] Carrying on like he is
inebriated, or high on the Most High, Crowder ap-
proaches blasphemy when he uses phrases like *"tokin'
the Ghost"* or *"having a little Jehovah-juana."*[18] Even
the humble-looking, low-key and soft-spoken Bill
Johnson of Bethel Church in Redding, California,
supports an *anointing* similar to that of Todd Bentley
in his congregational meetings (i.e., characterized by
drunken glory, fire tunnels, laughing, jerking, etc.).[19]

Critics (Justin Peters), skeptics (Carol Brooks),
and former members (Andrew Strom) liken the ecstatic manifestations of today's Prophetic Movement to the spiritual experiences associated with
the kundalini awakening in Hinduism, ancient
Eastern occultism and yoga. Kriyas (jerking),
laughter, touching the forehead in order to cause
a person to collapse (known as Shakti Pat), intense
emotional experiences, feelings of electricity, miracles and the attainment of spiritual knowledge are

17 "John Crowder—Ecstasy of God 1," YouTube video, posted by "GodofElijah," February 7, 2008, http://www.youtube.com/
watch?v=Ec91wvUY7Yo

18 "Shocking Documentary," YouTube video, posted by Andrew
Goodwin, December 13, 2011, www.youtube.com/watch?v=2X-
1HC-3s3uI

19 Steven Lambert, "Warning: Bill Johnson and Bethel Church," Spirit Life Magazine website, September 27, 2012, http://www.spiritlife-
mag.com/?p=2524

all well-documented aspects associated with the practice of Hindu gurus assisting spiritual seekers to awaken the kundalini (pictured as a coiled serpent) or corporeal energy within them so that they might attain enlightenment, self-realization and divine wisdom.[20]

Apparently, what is claimed to be a new work of God is actually an ancient move of Satan that has existed for thousands of years.

In fact, much of the teaching in the modern Prophetic Movement is akin to New Age philosophy. With their talk of guided visualization, acquiring spiritual knowledge through trances, spirit traveling, ecstatic or centering prayer, stigmata, bilocation and a preoccupation with angels, many branches of this Third Wave charismatic awakening look more like Hinduism and paganism than Christianity.

Watching video evidence of these neo-charismatic revival frontrunners leads one to conclude that these men and women seem to worship themselves as elite prophets more than they worship Jesus who is seated at the right hand of God. And they glorify their kooky experiences more than they glorify the almighty Creator. Yet their influence remains profound as they continue to spread this peculiar *anointing* all over the world.

20 "Slain in What Spirit, Part 1," InPlainSite.org, accessed December 15, 2012, http://www.inplainsite.org/html/slain_in_the_spirit_1.html

And it goes without saying that many of these neo-charismatic false teachers are extremely wealthy. In contrast to the lives of Christ and the early apostles, many of these modern hucksters enjoy lives of lavish opulence. They don't appear to be bearing any financial crosses for the cause of Christ.

Of course, that shouldn't surprise us. Because closely associated with the Word of Faith and the Apostolic-Prophetic movements is the third and final pillar of this most recent neo-charismatic splintering of evangelicalism—the Prosperity Gospel. Sometimes called the Health and Wealth Gospel, the message is always clear—financial and physical blessing *is* the will of God for all Christians.

In this teaching, believers are encouraged to access an assumed contract between man and God. The believer is taught to open the windows of heaven through faith, positive speech and, of course, donations to Christian ministries (sometimes called *seed money*). If humans have enough faith in God, he will deliver his promises of security and prosperity. The atonement is believed to include the alleviation of all sickness and poverty amongst God's children. Health and wealth are paralleled to the blessing of God. Sickness and poverty are linked to a lack of faith.

Some of the leading Prosperity Theology figures who have driven the movement include E. W. Kenyon, Oral Roberts, A. A. Allen, Robert Tilton, T. L. Osborn, Kenneth Hagin and Joel Osteen.

Word of Faith preachers Creflo Dollar, Kenneth
Copeland and Benny Hinn also obviously promote
the teaching.

Spread by televangelism, major Christian net-
works like TBN and the hungriness of the human
heart for wealth and physical comfort, Prosperity
Theology continues to swell.

> *By 2006, three of the four largest congrega-
> tions in the United States were teaching pros-
> perity theology, and Joel Osteen has been
> credited with spreading it outside of the Pente-
> costal and Charismatic movement through his
> books, which have sold over 4 million copies.*[21]

Kenneth Hagin summed up the movement
when he said, *"God is glorified through healing and
deliverance, not through sickness and suffering."*[22]
It's astounding and nauseating that a false teacher
can, in one sentence, attempt to wipe out the entire
God-centered life experience of a heroic Christian
sufferer like Joni Eareckson Tada. Based on a few
proof texts from Scripture, this particular brand of
false teaching continues to drain the pockets of the

---

21 "Prosperity theology," Wikipedia, accessed December 18, 2012,
http://en.wikipedia.org/wiki/Prosperity_theology

22 Nuggets of Wisdom, accessed on December 7, 2012, http://www.
savedhealed.com/nuggets.htm

naïve and discourage the terminally ill, who are rel-
egated to the dark corners of the crusade venues as
those lacking enough faith to see a miracle.

As I said, all three pillars of this neo-charismatic augmentation are closely related and often overlap (e.g., a Word of Faith preacher claiming to be
a modern day prophet delivers a health-and-wealth
message, earning a huge cut of the ridiculously large
offering collected that night after the sermon).

And all three pillars clearly display false Christian teaching. In Word of Faith, we see demonic
heresies that lead to a de-emphasis on the lordship
and supremacy of Christ. In the Prosperity Gospel,
we see the love of money, lack of personal account-
ability and a complete denial of the role of suffering
in the believer's life. And in the Apostolic-Prophetic
Movement, we see a lot of self-promotion, puffed
up arrogance and an over-crowded gallery of false
predictions and nutty behavior.

Listen to the apostle Peter writing almost 2,000
years ago. It sounds like he was able to peer directly
into contemporary Third Wave Pentecostalism:

> But there were also false prophets in Israel, just
> as there will be false teachers among you. They
> will cleverly teach destructive heresies and even
> deny the Master who bought them...Many will
> follow their evil teaching and shameful immo-
> rality. And because of these teachers, the way
> of truth will be slandered. In their greed they

will make up clever lies to get hold of your money...These people are proud and arrogant, daring even to scoff at supernatural beings without so much as trembling. But the angels, who are far greater in power and strength, do not dare to bring from the Lord a charge of blasphemy against those supernatural beings. These false teachers are like unthinking animals, creatures of instinct, born to be caught and destroyed. They scoff at things they do not understand, and like animals, they will be destroyed... They have wandered off the right road and followed the footsteps of Balaam son of Beor, who loved to earn money by doing wrong... These people are as useless as dried-up springs or as mist blown away by the wind. They are doomed to blackest darkness. They brag about themselves with empty, foolish boasting. (2 Peter 2:1–3, 10–12, 15, 17, 18)

Jesus himself cautioned potential followers about the dangers of counterfeit religious leaders, pretending to be something they aren't. *"Beware of false prophets who come disguised as harmless sheep but are really vicious wolves"* (Matthew 7:15). He also clearly taught us that miraculous manifestations are in no way the test of truth. *"For false messiahs and false prophets will rise up and perform signs and wonders so as to deceive, if possible, even God's chosen ones"* (Mark 13:22).

Perhaps many ministers in this realm of false teaching did not anticipate landing where they find themselves today. I imagine many began with honorable intentions and sincere motives but then became intoxicated with the money and power.

Consequently, today, what is called by many a *revival* within evangelicalism is, in fact, tantamount to rebellion against the Kingdom of God. What appears sacred by intent is actually seditious in nature. When scrutinizing these new movements, we need to ask ourselves, *What is being built here, the Kingdom of God or the empires of men?* Fidelity to God's Word is the ultimate test of true revival.

One final clarification—this chapter is not meant to be a downer on the power and gifts of the Holy Spirit, which I believe to be still functioning fully today in the promulgation of the gospel of Jesus Christ. This discussion should also not be taken as casting aspersions on orthodox Pentecostal assemblies. I don't want people to be suspicious of the true miracles of God that he performs in the establishment of his Kingdom all over the world. My passion is to warn eager and hungry seekers to tread carefully as they pursue signs and wonders that have no biblical basis and have little or nothing to do with the supremacy of Christ in the universe.

This most recent and radical fragmentation of evangelicalism has produced a host of religious figures and organizations that seem to be operating far from the reality of regular life and from the normal dynamics of meaningful relationships with friends and family. Even without the test of Scripture, the weird factor barometer in our souls should tell us to run from such nonsense so that we may avoid being deceived into potential sinful pursuits of God.

Right

As a general rule of thumb, it's better to spend more time talking about truth than dwelling on that which is false. Though last chapter's exposé might have seemed overly negative, consider it a necessary warning against theological strains that are, knowingly or unknowingly, leading the people of God into places he has not ordained.

The Bible is a storybook of pilgrims, young and old, pursuing God. As was discussed in the *Legacy* chapter, many people have sought to connect meaningfully with God by means of kindly human logic. The lesson we learn from them is that good intentions do not guarantee a deeper relationship with God. Religious passion and effort may appear good and helpful, but pursuing God in *truth* is all that really matters.

If we truly want to avoid a path of sacred sedition, of pursuing God sinfully, we can't just dwell on the bad; we must also pay close attention to those in the past who have done it right. What a joy now to consider biblical examples of the proper pursuit of God.

Fresh out of the Garden, the story of Cain and Abel teaches us that following God properly does not guarantee us a comfortable life. It cost Abel dearly to obey God and to offer suitable sacrifices to him. So we don't want to get the false impression that when we seek God rightly, everything will work out nicely here on earth. But as the New Testament explains, even though Abel's earthly life was tragically cut short by murder, he will stand forever in eternity as a member of God's righteous followers, approved by the Lord because of his obedient faith (Hebrews 11:4).

From the brief account of the life of Enoch, we learn that an intimate relationship with God comes from the practice of walking with him in a pleasing manner (Genesis 5:24). So many false paths to God involve rituals and behaviors that are either ascetic or absurd. How much simpler and yet profound to recognize the true godly path as one that involves a daily walk with the Lord, learning to discern his voice so we can obey him more consistently. Then at the end of our lives, each of us, like Enoch, may be *"known as a person who pleased God"* (Hebrews 11:5). Such rapport smacks of the original relationship humans enjoyed with God in the early days of the Garden.

When we consider the fascinating life of Noah, we also observe that walking with God can involve

significant personal sacrifice. Most likely subjected
to great ridicule along the way, Noah spent decades
building a large ocean-going vessel in the middle of
a plain. Every morning he woke up to the daunting
task of using simple hand tools to build a 450-foot-
long buoyant minivan while his neighbors jeered
and chuckled. But as a moral man amidst an entire world of wickedness, *"Noah found favor with
the Lord"* (Genesis 6:8). The writer of Genesis said,
*"Noah was a righteous man, the only blameless per-
son living on earth at the time, and he walked in close
fellowship with God"* (Genesis 6:9). Again we see
that one who walks closely with God is focused only
on obeying all that the Lord says—*"So Noah did everything as the Lord commanded him"* (Genesis 7:5).

One cannot discuss pursuing God rightly without revisiting Abraham. Though his sinful behavior
with Hagar illustrates a major blip on his faith radar, Abraham's life in its entirety stands as a powerful example of how to develop a proper relationship
with God. Though not perfect, this father of faith
was willing to do extraordinary things in obedience
to God. With no clue of where he was going, Abraham left the comforts and familiarities of his home
country to settle in a far-away land that God had
promised for his future ancestors. He also believed
God could miraculously produce an heir out of really old people who were *"as good as dead"* (Hebrews
11:12). And by the climax of his walk with the Lord,
Abraham even believed God would raise Isaac back

to life if he died on the sacrificial altar at the top of Mount Moriah (Hebrews 11:19).

The Scriptures are very clear regarding the fact that Abraham was declared righteous and was justified before God because of his faith (Genesis 15:6; Romans 4:3). But unlike Word of Faith proponents today who occupy themselves with notions of health and wealth creation, Abraham's faith was solidly rooted in God's revealed Word. All that mattered was whether or not he believed and obeyed what God told him to do. And because of his commitment to trust and follow the Lord, Abraham became the father of all who believe and cultivate *"a right relationship with God that comes by faith"* (Romans 4:13).

Third in the ancestral line of Abraham, Joseph would have made his great-grandpa proud. This patriarch's strong relationship with God was most evident in his devotion to personal holiness. Facing a temptation many men would have embraced, Joseph told Potiphar's wife that to sleep with her would not only be a violation of his master's trust, *"It would be a great sin against God"* (Genesis 39:9). Those who desire to pursue God, God's way, do not underestimate the power of depravity in their lives. They recognize sin's wily tactics and its utter and putrid defilement of God's holiness. Hence the need to flee from it, as Joseph so aptly modeled for us (Genesis 39:12).

Throughout his adult life, Joseph continued to exemplify the proper pursuit of God through his prudent behavior. When wrongfully accused, he left his defense in God's hands. When subjected to a lengthy and uncomfortable prison sentence, Joseph remained positive and productive, showing interest in other people's problems (i.e., Pharaoh's baker and cup-bearer). When forgotten by the world, he remembered to remain faithful to the Lord. When opportunities for political and historical impact arose, Joseph was prepared to step forward and use the gifts that God had blessed him with. When given the chance to pour scathing revenge upon his brothers for their dastardly deed of betrayal, Joseph chose to forgive. He also elected to see the sovereign hand of God at work through the misfortunes of his life. In so many ways, Joseph exhibited the true way to follow hard after God.

As did Moses. The author of Hebrews summarized this great prophet's life in the following manner:

It was by faith that Moses, when he grew up, refused to be called the son of Pharaoh's daughter. He chose to share the oppression of God's people instead of enjoying the fleeting pleasures of sin. He thought it was better to suffer for the sake of Christ than to own the treasures of Egypt, for he was looking ahead to his great reward. It was by faith that Moses left the land of Egypt, not fearing the king's anger. He kept right on going because he kept his eyes on the one who is invisible. (Hebrews 11:24–27)

Moses' life demonstrated many of the hallmarks of a right relationship with God—separation from the world, abhorrence of sin, valuing suffering over material possessions, fearing God more than man and exercising great power in accordance with the Word of God.

Moses' protégé adopted many of the faithful practices of his mentor. In the life of Joshua we see that when we want to obey God fully and believe his every promise, we will undoubtedly face formidable opposition (i.e., the other ten spies and all the nation of Israel). To go God's way often involves paddling against the stream of popularity.

But Joshua's life also teaches us that faithful obedience to God can bring down some pretty big walls of resistance to our spiritual growth (i.e., Jericho and the entire conquest of the Promised Land being a prophetic type or symbol of the attainment of victorious Christian living).

Many other Old Testament characters offer valuable insight into this matter of properly pursuing God.

Rahab, for instance, shows us the importance of being able to discern between the true power of Yahweh and the deceptive power of false gods (Joshua 2:10–11).

The story of Gideon teaches us that rightly following the Lord involves learning to do great things in God's power as opposed to our own human strength.

The life of Ruth exemplifies how a true believer survives personal tragedy by abandoning bitterness and idolatry in favor of faithfully clinging to God and caring for others in need (i.e., her bereaved mother-in-law). In Ruth's case, she walked in faith into a new land where she discovered a tender and compassionate savior (Boaz) she didn't even know existed.

From the psalmist David, we learn that those who seek the Lord in truth can experience many setbacks in their lives. But even though assailants abound on every side, a faithful heart is still able to sing praises to God (Psalm 59) and maintain its trust in the omnipresent and omniscient Creator (Psalm 139). Also in this godly king's life, we see the utmost importance of Scripture (Psalm 119), confession of sin (Psalm 32) and a broken, contrite heart (Psalm 51). David's passion for God could be summed up in the first verse of Psalm 63—*"O God, you are my God; I earnestly search for you. My soul thirsts for you; my whole body longs for you."*

In the life of Isaiah we see that those who genuinely follow God understand their own sinfulness as the ruinous cause of their natural separation from his spectacular holiness (Isaiah 6:1–5). As well, Isaiah shows us that those who are fully surrendered to God are willing to tell God's message to whomever needs to hear it (Isaiah 6:8–13).

The story of the prophet Daniel epitomizes a life of faithfulness to God in the midst of a pagan culture. As a young man ripped away from all parental and community support, Daniel showed exceptional strength and character. He understood the importance of abstaining from food and drink associated with pagan or demonic rituals (Daniel 1:8). As he submitted to God's laws and studied diligently in preparation for royal service, God blessed him with wisdom far beyond his Babylonian peers (Daniel 1:20).

And even though Daniel experienced spectacular visions and prophetic dreams that told of future times, his wholehearted devotion to God was evident by his humility and complete integrity. Promotions did come to him, but always from the hand of God, not because he connived his way to the top. When his jealous colleagues tried to bring him down, *"they couldn't find anything to criticize or condemn. He was faithful, always responsible, and completely trustworthy"* (Daniel 6:4). If only today's televangelists could have the same reputation.

As remarkable as they were, every example of faithfulness and obedience in the Old Testament era ends up paling in comparison to the pristine life of the Son of God.

Through the incarnation of our Lord Jesus Christ, the world was finally able to see the most complete revelation of God himself (Hebrews 1:1–3). Finally, a picture of pure devotion to God had arrived. Jesus lived a life of perfect obedience and showed us what total reliance on the Father looks like. Luke summarized our Lord's earthly ministry by simply saying, *"Jesus went around doing good"* (Acts 10:38).

Though he performed countless signs and wonders, bringing health and relief to many of his countrymen, Christ always downplayed the miraculous as secondary. His demonstrations of power were never considered an end in themselves. The miracles he performed were solely for the purpose of authenticating his role as the promised Messiah (Luke 4:16–19).

Jesus told his disciples that their salvation was more important than their power over demons. *"But don't rejoice because evil spirits obey you; rejoice because your names are registered in heaven"* (Luke 10:20). He also made it very clear that doing the will of God—displaying good fruit—always trumps a miracle show. For on the Day of Judgment, many people will claim to have done supernatural phenomena in Jesus' name but will be barred from the Kingdom because of their disobedience and lack of relationship with Christ (Matthew 7:21–23). Jesus also predicted that in the end times leading up to his second coming, false prophets will perform great signs and wonders as a form of spiritual deception (Matthew 24:24). In fact, Jesus labeled the people who typically ask for signs as evil and adulterous (Matthew 16:4).

Years later, the apostle Paul, as well, criticized his countrymen for always wanting to see signs (1 Corinthians 1:22). For he knew, like Jesus, that miracles play a very small role in the matter of truly connecting with God. The weight of New Testament teaching regarding this topic tips heavily in favor of visible fruit. In the words of Jesus, *"Yes, just as you can identify a tree by its fruit, so you can identify people by their actions"* (Matthew 7:20).

Outward miracles may initially bring someone to Christ, but it is the inward work of the Holy Spirit that transforms the true children of God into the likeness of Christ. In other words, as was seen in the life of Jesus, true believers demonstrate the fruit of the Spirit—love, joy, peace, patience, kindness, goodness, faithfulness, gentleness and self-control (Galatians 5:22–23).

The message of the New Testament stands apart from the nonsense promoted in the miracle-seeking Prophetic Movement of our contemporary world. You see, the problem with outward miracles is that they don't really fix what's broken. Lazarus eventually died again. Participants at the feeding of the 5,000 needed food the next day. Nine of the ten cleansed lepers walked away from Jesus and continued in their sinful ways.

The true brokenness of the human soul is rooted in our sin problem. This is what needs to be fixed. We are stubborn and selfish. We want our own way and feel bugged when we don't get it. Even when we seek God with great vigor, we are tempted to do it our own way.

That is why Peter proclaimed his famous words on the Day of Pentecost. After the mighty wind and the miraculous display of fire and speaking in tongues, Peter delivered a rousing sermon to the awestruck Jewish crowd. At the end of his rebuke for their crucifixion of Christ, they were pierced to the heart, *"and they said to him and to the other apostles, 'Brothers, what should we do?'"* (Acts 2:37). Peter appropriately replied with an exhortation to repent. There was no encouragement to seek more miracles for their personal benefit, just a call to repentance.

John the Baptist gave the same plea when people came out to the wilderness to hear him preach, wanting to get their lives right with God in preparation for his Kingdom (Matthew 3:2). New life in Christ always starts and continues with repentance. Unlike *revivals* today that showcase spectacular manifestations and a lot of noise, true revival always involves some form of repentance.

Repentance literally means *a change of mind.* Those who want to come to God on his terms must start with a change of mind about many things. First, there must be a change of mind regarding the matter of personal independence and self-reliance. One who truly seeks God must come with an attitude of total submission and surrender. Regeneration is not a self-help project; nor does God operate as a renovation partner in the reconstruction of our souls. It is God who saves and sanctifies. Our job is to trust him and obey his instructions for life.

But true repentance consists of other aspects as well. It involves a change of mind about the seriousness of sin and the need for a Savior. There must also be new thinking about the supreme holiness of God and how becoming his child welcomes certain claims on our lives. And finally, there is need for a radical revolution regarding almost every aspect of natural human behavior.

Where the unregenerate thinks first of himself, the saved soul is expected to consider the needs of others as primary. Everything the world claims as being great (money, power and status) is turned upside down by the Christian paradigm. The first will be last and the last first. True greatness is demonstrated by servanthood. Christ was glorified by death on a criminal's cross. Instead of celebrating regal displays of grandiose strength and ostentatious achievement, God's Kingdom values mourning, meekness, mercy, purity, peace, a hunger for righteousness and suffering for godly living (Matthew 5:1–12).

And no other person in the New Testament, besides Christ, embodied this radical Kingdom life better than the apostle Paul. His story epitomizes doing it right. After his divine encounter on the road to Damascus, Paul gave up his life of privilege and position to be numbered among those humiliated for the cause of Christ.

Because of his calling and devotion to God, as well as his deep love for people, he worked tirelessly to preach the gospel while maintaining his tentmaker trade on the side to pay his own way on missionary journeys. He pleaded for people to respond to his message of reconciliation to God. He prayed for people unceasingly. He wept for their souls. But instead of warm receptions and appreciation for his efforts, Paul endured great hardship with many imprisonments. Numerous times he was beaten with fists, rods and whips. Once he was even stoned and left for dead. In his own words, *"For I bear on my body the scars that show I belong to Jesus"* (Galatians 6:17).

Paul endured dangers in his travels from every angle. If the Jews weren't hounding him, it was the Gentile authorities. If it wasn't the Gentiles, false teachers harassed him and slipped into his churches after he left in order to discredit his ministry and destroy his work. Many times he endured hunger, thirst, sleepless nights and exposure from the cold, all for the sake of the gospel of Christ.

As he was approaching his physical death, Paul referred to his life as having *"already been poured out as an offering to God"* (2 Timothy 4:6). In many ways, this phrase is a perfect summary of what it means to properly pursue God. Unlike the false teachers of today who shamelessly market their Prosperity Gospel wares, Paul taught us that those who want to have a genuine relationship with God must empty their lives of all self-ambition and pretentious piety. Those who want to do it right must humbly present everything they are and have as an offering to God.

And Paul makes it very clear that this life of sacrifice is not a pathetic pointless endeavor or a morose existence of self-pity. It is a spectacular life of human brokenness that ends victoriously—with Christ in glory. Listen to how he explained it to the church at Corinth:

You see, we don't go around preaching about ourselves. We preach that Jesus Christ is Lord, and we ourselves are your servants for Jesus' sake. For God, who said, "Let there be light in the darkness," has made this light shine in our hearts so we could know the glory of God that is seen in the face of Jesus Christ.

We now have this light shining in our hearts, but we ourselves are like fragile clay jars containing this great treasure. This makes it clear that our great power is from God, not from ourselves.

We are pressed on every side by troubles, but we are not crushed. We are perplexed, but not driven to despair. We are hunted down, but never abandoned by God. We get knocked down, but we are not destroyed. Through suffering, our bodies continue to share in the death of Jesus so that the life of Jesus may also be seen in our bodies.

Yes, we live under constant danger of death because we serve Jesus, so that the life of Jesus will be evident in our dying bodies. So we live in the face of death, but this has resulted in eternal life for you.

But we continue to preach because we have the same kind of faith the psalmist had when he said, "I believed in God, so I spoke." We know that God, who raised the Lord Jesus, will also raise us with Jesus and present us to himself together with you. All of this is for your benefit. And as God's grace reaches more and more people, there will be great thanksgiving, and God will receive more and more glory.

That is why we never give up. Though our bodies are dying, our spirits are being renewed every day. For our present troubles are small and won't last very long. Yet they produce for us a glory that vastly outweighs them and will last forever! So we don't look at the troubles we can see now; rather, we fix our gaze on things that cannot be seen. For the things we see now will soon be gone, but the things we cannot see will last forever. (2 Corinthians 4:5–18)

As we seek for common threads in the narratives of this chapter, several aspects rise to the fore. Those who seek the Lord in truth must start from a vantage point of absolute faith in God. All self-reliance must be abandoned.

Next, there needs to be a sincere confession of sin and a significant recognition of the holiness of God. The lives of those doing it right will be characterized primarily by purity, self-sacrifice, submission and obedience to the revealed Word of God. Their Christian experience will resemble a daily walk of consistent and faithful reverence for truth as they fellowship personally with the God of the universe.

There will also be far more fear of God in their lives than fear of man. The by-product of their Christian walk will taste like the fruit of the Spirit. And they will not shy away from hardship or suffering for the cause of Christ, because they will see the purpose of their lives as being broken vessels that spill out the grace of the Lord Jesus Christ, all for the glory of God.

This is what it looks like to do it right.

Christ

As we begin the final chapter of our journey, it's time to talk bottom line—whoever desires to enter into a true relationship with God must do so through Jesus Christ. Our Lord stated it plainly to his disciples in the final days before his crucifixion: *"I am the way, the truth, and the life. No one can come to the Father except through me"* (John 14:6). Any other path is seditious and subversive, no matter how sincere or sacred sounding.

If any part of the journey to God contradicts the teaching or character of Christ, it should be considered suspect. Behaviors or spiritual manifestations that lead one away from Christlikeness probably originate from the world, the flesh or the devil, as opposed to the Holy Spirit. To attribute all spiritual phenomena to the Holy Spirit is to walk on very shaky ground. The abundance of scriptural warnings regarding the need for spiritual discernment points to the existence of counterfeits.

The Bible says that the Holy Spirit works in ways that glorify Christ (John 16:14). And when the Spirit speaks to us, he is only saying things that he has heard from the other members of the Trinity (John 16:13). He has no agenda other than to bear witness of Christ (John 15:26) and to build his church through conforming us into the image of Jesus (Galatians 5:22–23). It makes no sense to equate the fullness of the Spirit with bizarre exhibitions or showy displays of the flesh. He is not some random spiritual force or energy field dedicated to making us feel good or warm all over. Pleasurable feelings cannot automatically be equated with pure and undefiled love for God. A lot of *show* does not necessarily mean that *God really showed up today* in church.

We are in theological and practical error to reduce the fullness of the Spirit to one small aspect of the Spirit's work as displayed in the book of Acts. For example, to equate the filling of the Holy Spirit solely with the gift of tongues is to do a complete injustice to him and the Scriptures as a whole. We need to see the fullness of the Holy Spirit in all its fullness.

The concept shows up first in the book of Acts. In this account of the early church, the fullness of the Spirit resulted in at least fifteen different manifestations. In Acts 1:8, Jesus promised his disciples a new kind of power when the Holy Spirit was to come upon them. In Acts 2, the infilling of the Holy Spirit resulted in the speaking of other languages, clearly for the purpose of glorifying God by praising him for his mighty deeds. In Acts 4:8, the fullness of the Spirit catapulted Peter into a great sermon. In Acts 4:31–32, the body of believers who were filled with the Holy Spirit spoke the Word of God with boldness, became strongly unified and started acting abnormally charitable towards those in need.

In Acts 6, we meet Stephen, whose Spirit-filled life was characterized by wisdom and faith. When this very same Stephen was filled with the Holy Spirit in Acts 7, he received a vision of heaven, courage to face death and the ability to forgive his murderers. In Acts 9, we see the fullness of the Spirit launching the apostle Paul into his full-time ministry. Acts 11:24 describes Barnabas as *"a good man, full of the Holy Spirit and strong in faith."* In Acts 13:9, the fullness of the Spirit gave Paul the ability to discern the work of evil spirits. And in Acts 13:53, the fullness of the Spirit gave great joy to the believers.

So the Holy Spirit's fullness manifested itself in many ways in the early church, always providing whatever was needed for the work of the Kingdom of God in each particular situation. Whether that meant fulfilling an Old Testament prophecy by speaking to the Jews in other languages at Pentecost (Isaiah 28:11; cf. 1 Corinthians 14:21) or empowering a believer to face death courageously, the Holy Spirit's full presence was always directed towards the building of the church. Christ said, *"I will build my church, and all the powers of hell will not conquer it"* (Matthew 16:18). The Holy Spirit is dedicated to the execution of this plan. He has no desire to perform freakish displays or crowd-pleasing parlor tricks just for kicks.

In the grand scheme of God revealing himself to man throughout history, Pentecost is certainly a watershed. The Holy Spirit came to believers in a new way at Pentecost, but his focus was, and still is, Jesus. It's worth repeating—John's Gospel says that the Spirit glorifies Jesus and reveals to us only what Jesus tells him. Consequently, the Spirit does nothing silly; nor does he have any desire to bring attention to himself or us. It's all about Christ and his work of building his church. Any words, actions or decisions supposedly made under the infilling of the Holy Spirit that do otherwise are part of a different gospel than the one Christ and his apostles preached.

When you look at the Scriptures as a whole, it becomes quite clear that the presence of the Holy Spirit in the life of a believer is the same concept as the *indwelling Christ* that Paul talks about in Galatians 2:20. Yes, the Spirit gives necessary gifts to build and strengthen the church so that it may function properly and successfully, but the fullness of the Spirit cannot produce anything other than the character of Christ—that's his job. It's no surprise then that the fruit of the Spirit is simply Christlike character, the stuff that can't be faked. We cannot lose sight of the big idea that Holy Spirit fullness essentially equals Christlikeness. It does not equal weirdness or confusion or a load of artificial hype.

When the primary focus of spiritual seekers is on signs and wonders, people regularly fall for imitations of that which is genuine. Disguising himself as an angel of light, Satan mimics miracles that entertain the flesh but sidetrack us from attaining Christian maturity. Authentic spiritual growth often does include outward miracles, but most of the Spirit's work in a believer's life is unseen. Through inner transformation and the gifts that strengthen the church body (e.g., teaching, serving, encouraging), the Holy Spirit works to bear in us the fruit of godly character—Christlikeness.

Even a cursory reading of Paul's letters to the churches at Ephesus and Colossae reveals the truth that God has nothing to give us beyond Jesus Christ.

From Ephesians, we learn that Christ is the source of every spiritual blessing (1:3), the conduit through which we are adopted as God's children (1:5), the foundation of our redemption and forgiveness (1:7), the basis of Christian unity (2:11–16) and the chief cornerstone of God's household (2:19–20). Because of our association with Christ, we receive the Holy Spirit as a guarantee that our Heavenly Father is going to give us a marvelous inheritance in the future (1:11, 13, 14).

As a result of the Father's delight in the good work of his Son, God raised Jesus from the dead and seated him at his right hand, far above all rulers, authorities and powers (1:20–21). From this exalted position, Christ authoritatively rules over everything in the universe and acts as head of all things for the benefit of the church (1:10, 22). The apostle Paul concluded the chapter with the following words: *"And the church is his body; it is made full and complete by Christ, who fills all things everywhere with himself"* (1:23).

The apostolic writer wanted his readers to get the point—everything that pertains to God is found in the Son. He alone is the source of all true spiritual growth. Again, God has nothing to give us beyond Jesus Christ.

In the Epistle to the Colossians, Paul further expanded his argument. Christ is not only the visible image of the invisible God, he is the agent through whom God created all things both visible and invisible (1:15–16). By the word of his power, Christ holds everything in creation together, every second of every day (1:17). And it is through his blood on the cross that a fallen world can find peace and reconciliation with God (1:20). Rightly so, at the end of the story Christ assumes first place in everything according to the Father's plan (1:18).

To sum up, Paul said, *"For God in all his fullness was pleased to live in Christ"* (1:19). That is why the apostle strongly stated his single purpose in life to be the declaration of Christ—*"We proclaim Him, admonishing every man and teaching every man with all wisdom, so that we may present every man complete in Christ"* (1:28, NASB). *"Growth which is from God"* comes only through *"holding fast to the head"* (2:19, NASB).

Even in the first century, Paul recognized the primary tactic of our spiritual enemy—to demean the supremacy of Christ and to draw us away from him as the source of all spiritual growth.

> *I am telling you this so no one will deceive you with well-crafted arguments…just as you accepted Christ Jesus as your Lord, you must continue to follow him. Let your roots grow down into him, and let your lives be built on him. Then your faith will grow strong in the truth you were taught, and you will overflow with thankfulness. Don't let anyone capture you with empty philosophies and high-sounding nonsense that come from human thinking and from the spiritual powers of this world, rather than from Christ. For in Christ lives all the fullness of God in a human body. So you also are complete through your union with Christ, who is the head over every ruler and authority.* (Colossians 2:4, 6–10)

You'd have to be in a coma to miss it—pursuing God, God's way, absolutely implies proceeding in and through Jesus Christ. There is no other way, period! If the Bible remains our authority for truth, there can be no doubt about this matter.

Yet many claim to be following Jesus as they pursue pathways to God that display no obvious Christlike markings. The true test of following Jesus is based not on words that proceed from the mouth but on deeds done in the body. We can repeatedly refer to Jesus as *"Lord, Lord"* but still end up outside the Kingdom because, in the words of Christ, we have neglected to *"actually do the will of my Father in heaven"* (Matthew 7:21).

We can speak the name of Jesus all we like as we practice our self-made religions, but there is no mistaking the true path to God through Christ as taught in Scripture. Not only is it clearly delineated in the words of Jesus and the apostolic writers, it was modeled for us by Christ himself. Those who want to get to God must walk the path Christ walked.

First of all, the way to God through Jesus is a hard way. Our Lord himself made this very clear. To follow him involves a substantial cost, one that should be considered before we embark on the journey of becoming his disciples (Luke 14:28). Following Christ involves surrender and submission, obedience and self-denial. He called the wealthy to give up all their possessions and the powerful to behave like servants.

In his own life, he was found fully faithful and obedient to his Father's will. Having *"learned obedience from the things he suffered"* (Hebrews 5:8), the elevated Christ is now a demanding master himself, laying down tough stipulations for his followers—*"Be perfect, even as your Father in heaven is perfect"* (Matthew 5:48). To truly love Christ is to elevate him far above the level of commitment and affection we have for our own family members (Luke 14:26). The cost to follow him to God is not cheap.

Secondly, the way to God through Jesus is a narrow way. If we truly intend to connect with God, we need to go where the crowds aren't. Jesus said,

> *You can enter God's Kingdom only through the narrow gate. The highway to hell is broad, and its gate is wide for the many who choose that way. But the gateway to life is very narrow and the road is difficult, and only a few ever find it.* (Matthew 7:13–14)

During his earthly ministry, Jesus seemed to favor making personal connections with individual people. When there was an opportunity to bolster general crowd support for his ministry, he discouraged it. He regularly forbade those he healed from telling others about their miracles.

Unlike the showmen of today's Prophetic Movement, Jesus knew that miracle madness only causes a distracting frenzy of excitement that is more fleshly than spiritual. Where there are lots of people with high levels of excitement, there is a good chance that very little true Kingdom work is transpiring (e.g., the crowds who chased Jesus for another meal after he fed the 5,000). Christ's work was never about running a popularity contest. The way to God is a narrow way with fewer genuine participants than you'd expect.

But it's also a way of delayed reward. The way to God through Jesus includes experiencing a cross before receiving a crown. The promises of eternal life, godly inheritance and Kingdom rule are exciting, but their fulfillment is largely in the future. As Christ exemplified for us, our present earthy dwelling experience is filled with much trouble and sorrow. Unlike today's Prosperity Gospel preachers who promise instant gratification for all our desires, Jesus said he didn't even have a place to call home, where he could just lay his head down and rest. Christ's message to us now is to store up all our treasure in heaven for a future reward (Matthew 6:20).

Though he wrote almost 2,000 years ago, the apostle Paul correctly prophesied,

> *For a time is coming when people will no longer listen to sound and wholesome teaching. They will follow their own desires and will look for teachers who will tell them whatever their itching ears want to hear. They will reject the truth and chase after myths.* (2 Timothy 4:3–4)

People would rather follow strange myths than hear about dying to self. People prefer having their ears tickled to listening to a *no rights* speech. But the truth is still the truth. A relationship with Jesus Christ is the only way to eternal life, and Jesus promised his true followers persecution (2 Timothy 3:12) and suffering (Philippians 1:29; 1 Peter 2:21).

Christ also promised his followers a daily burden to bear:

> *If any of you wants to be my follower, you must turn from your selfish ways, take up your cross daily, and follow me. If you try to hang on to your life, you will lose it. But if you give up your life for my sake, you will save it.* (Luke 9:23–24)

Christ himself bore a cross before earning his crown. How can we expect anything different as his followers?

Count the cost. Hunt for the narrow gate at the end of the difficult road. Daily bear your cross by dying to self. This is the way to God. The hard way is the right way.

But it's not a road of hardship without purpose, as an existentialist might claim. The suffering that God allows for his children on their journey to him is a calculated conditioning of character. The cross that we bear ends up bearing fruit in our lives. It truly is a hardship-to-hope story. Paul explained it this way to the church at Rome:

We can rejoice, too, when we run into problems and trials, for we know that they help us develop endurance. And endurance develops strength of character, and character strengthens our confident hope of salvation. And this hope will not lead to disappointment. For we know how dearly God loves us, because he has given us the Holy Spirit to fill our hearts with his love. When we were utterly helpless, Christ came at just the right time and died for us sinners…So now we can rejoice in our wonderful new relationship with God because our Lord Jesus Christ has made us friends of God.
(Romans 5:3–6, 11)

Indeed, it is Jesus, and Jesus alone, who makes us friends with God. And he does so as we follow him with all our hearts. We cannot merely be fans who cheer him on from the sidelines at the big game. We need to be tracking and imitating Christ continually. Fans of Christ who focus on spiritual gifts or miraculous manifestations as ends in themselves inevitably get distracted. And this distraction often leads them into deception of the weirdest kind. Wholly intent on shadowing and obeying their master, followers keep their eyes on Jesus. Fans are looking somewhere else.

It truly is all about Jesus. Not because he is a megalomaniac or a self-absorbed deity, but because he is the Son of God. The Father's plan of salvation and redemption was carried out by the Son. And the Son gets to lead many other sons to glory. The writer of Hebrews stated it plainly:

> *God, for whom and through whom everything was made, chose to bring many children into glory. And it was only right that he should make Jesus, through his suffering, a perfect leader, fit to bring them into their salvation.* (Hebrews 2:10)

Jesus, as the conductor of this little band marching to glory, will provide what is needed for the journey. He will lead with perfect timing and flawless dynamics. He will only give directions that reflect his nature and character. And he will only take us to places that the Father has prescribed.

If we are traveling in the proper lane of pursuing God, we will know that the Father has nothing to give us beyond Jesus Christ. The vehicles in the other lanes have *Sacred Sedition* on their license plates.

Reflection

CREATION LONGS TO BE IN RIGHT RELATIONSHIP WITH its creator. The hunger in the human heart for meaning and purpose is only satisfied through an intimate connection with God. Most sincere spiritual seekers can agree on that. Where disagreement arises is in the manner of attaining such an intimate connection.

A few years ago, I bought a beautiful cherrywood desk for my study. It was a large structure requiring home assembly, arriving in three huge boxes, weighing over 500 pounds. As I started to pull the pieces out of the boxes, I slipped into my usual habit. Instead of hunting for the instructions, I defaulted to my razor-sharp human intellect to decide how the myriad pieces of wood and steel should best fit together. You can probably guess how that turned out.

Eventually, I submitted my rational thought to the manufacturer's assembly manual.

We are fooling ourselves to believe that good intentions and dedicated energy are the sole requirements for achieving a close relationship with God. Truly, sincerity and effort are essential, but they need to be guided by submission to God and obedience to his Word.

It may sound hokey, but it wouldn't be wrong to call the Bible the *Owner's Manual for Life*. Many God-seekers are tempted to set aside the manual and piece together their life journey to our Heavenly Father based on their own theories of spiritual growth. Many other pursuers of the Almighty, with little knowledge of the manual, end up deceived by false teachers who twist the Scriptures for their own personal gain.

We started our discussion with a question—*Is it ever right to disobey God in order to be closer to God?* At first glance, the question seems to be rhetorical. But when we study the lives of spiritual seekers in the Scriptures and examine our own lives, we see that the answer to this question is not so obvious. In reality, countless people throughout all of history have essentially answered this question affirmatively.

Without realizing it, those who believe they can find their own way to God are susceptible to the practice of sacred sedition. Even though their motives seem holy, their failure to humble themselves to God's instruction makes their behavior rebellious. Sedition doesn't have to be noisy to be seditious.

Rebellion is often subtle and insidious. Attempting to come to God outside of an immersion into the life of Christ is a path of attempted holiness based on human insight. Such a path of sacred sedition quietly leads one to destruction.

And we cannot ignore the fact that sacred sedition is often the product of spiritual deception. The Bible speaks so much about this topic, we dare not ignore it. Daily, we need to guard our fickle hearts from being lured away by spiritual shortcuts or heretical emotional attractions. Daily we need to bathe our minds in Scripture so we can discern the truth about knowing God personally through his son Jesus. Moment by moment, we need to recognize the reality of demonic forces, the lures of worldliness and the stinking selfishness of our own sinful flesh—the forces that work against a true intimate connection with God.

It is a great and noble desire to be closer to God. *"The Lord looks down from heaven...to see... if anyone seeks God"* (Psalm 14:2). There is no truer purpose in life. Yet it is important to understand that such a pursuit will be tainted by sin if it is guided solely by human intuition.

Pursuing God in our own way is simply another form of human self-centeredness. If we are not prepared to totally humble ourselves and approach God in the manner that he has clearly prescribed, we are no better off than agnostics or atheists. In fact, we may even be worse off because we think we're on the straight and narrow when we're actually on the broad path that leads to destruction.

Those who desire to pursue God must do so his way.

Dwight Olney grew up in Kitchener, Ontario, as the son of a piano tuner. At fifteen, he moved to Alberta when his father returned to his pastoral calling by taking a church in the small northern community of Lac La Biche. After high school, Dwight trained to become a secondary teacher, focusing on history and mathematics. Currently, he works as an in-school administrator for the Prairie South School Division in southern Saskatchewan. All told, Dwight has spent thirty years in the field of education.

He has studied theology (Briercrest College), history (University of Waterloo), education (Queen's University) and administration (Jones International University). Dwight loves teaching, preaching, trumpet-playing, carpentry, playing tennis, recreational hockey and coaching basketball. He has three grown children and lives with his wife, Jeanette, in Caronport, Saskatchewan.

Throughout his adult life, Dwight has enjoyed studying and teaching the Bible as an adult Sunday school teacher, a preacher and a principal of a private Christian high school. His fondest area of interest is practical theology. He loves to challenge people to think in new ways by recognizing faulty human thought lines and replacing them with God-like thinking.

Sacred Sedition is Dwight's third book, following on the heels of *Master Mind: Thinking Like God* (2009) and its sequel, *Mind Renovation* (2011).

www.ingramcontent.com/pod-product-compliance
Lightning Source LLC
Chambersburg PA
CBHW061823040426
42447CB00012B/2790